OLYMPIC GYMNASTICS FOR SCHOOLS

Olympic Gymnastics for Schools

Walter G. Dunn

PELHAM BOOKS

First published in Great Britain by
PELHAM BOOKS LTD
26 Bloomsbury Street,
London, W.C.1
1969

0 7207 0174 0

Printed in Great Britain by
Northumberland Press Limited
Gateshead

CONTENTS

ILLUSTRATIONS

Photographs

7

Drawings

ONE

INTRODUCTION TO OLYMPIC GYMNASTICS

It was Shakespeare who said, speaking through the mouth of Hamlet, 'What a piece of work is a man! how noble in reason! how infinite in faculty! in form, in moving, how express and admirable! in action how like an angel! in apprehension how like a god! the beauty of the world! the paragon of animals!'

How much more impressed would Shakespeare have been could he have been present at the recent International Gymnastic Championships and witnessed the beauty of form and exquisite movement of the world's top gymnasts! He would without question have realised how true his words really were, for here indeed was the very quintessence of perfection in movement; of grace and beauty beyond compare; of exquisite action and breath-taking feats sufficient to quicken the pulses and stir the imagination of the most critical perfectionist. The young performers were in truth 'express and admirable' if not 'angels in action', and certainly an example to our country where, regretfully, mediocrity is being accepted as the peak of perfection as regards gymnastic performance.

Sad to relate, there was not a single member of the Commonwealth taking part in that most auspicious event.

It is evident from the appreciative comments one hears from members of the public following a television broadcast of gymnastics that such programmes have a wide appeal and would attract a much greater following if presented more frequently and if the Press gave more space to the sport. One cannot altogether blame these agencies for failing to publicise gymnastics for very little is being done by education authorities, gymnastic organisations and other sporting bodies to give the sport the prominence it deserves.

What, one may ask, is the role of gymnastics in schools today? In most schools it occupies a very minor role. The accent is more on general activities which do not demand such a high degree of co-ordination and training as gymnastics does. In Olympic gymnastics the situation is much more serious for in few schools is this attractive but demanding aspect of gymnastics practised at all.

There are, of course, certain limiting factors which preclude the inclusion of Olympic gymnastics in schools' programmes. Chief among these is the very serious shortage of teachers with the ability, training and keenness to teach the sport – even at a low level of performance. However, it is possible to overcome this deficiency by implementing some of the following measures:

1. There is an untapped reservoir of highly skilled gymnastic performers leaving the Services each year. Many of these trained instructors seek employment in schools and colleges but very few are successful because they lack the educational qualifications or professional training in a college-of-education to satisfy the demands of the authorities. Surely a great number of these instructors could be given a short one-year course in a college-of-education in the same way as qualified tradesmen are given such an opportunity of qualifying as teachers. Again, many student teachers are nowadays being accepted for training with little, if any, academic qualifications.

In my opinion such experts would give physical education a much needed stimulus and their exclusion from teaching in schools and colleges is a wanton waste of much needed expertise and excellent talent. The fine displays given by gymnastic teams from the three Services are ample evidence in support of my contention, and proof of the high standard of training that these men receive.

2. More emphasis must be placed on training gymnastic specialists in colleges of education and in specialist P.E. colleges. In fact, because of the wide variety of activities which P.E. specialists are expected to cope with, it might be worth considering running parallel courses for such specialists one course catering for gymnastics and athletics, and the other for games and outdoor activities.

Of course there would be an overlap of interests but it must be recognised that top experts in teaching advanced gymnastics are not always good games players and, by the same token, good games coaches are seldom top gymnastic teachers. There are of course exceptions to this but it is true to say that at present, P.E. men are bound to become Jacks of all trades.

In fact, the role of the P.E. teacher has now become that of a play supervisor, an organiser and administrator perhaps, but seldom engaged in vital, concentrated coaching and teaching sessions.

3. The physical-education programme, instead of being a hotch-potch of physical activities, should be clearly defined so that educational gymnastics (including Olympic gymnastics) and systematised exercise, having specific developmental and corrective effects, should form the essential core of the physical-education programme. Games sessions should be occupied by games coaching and the practise of skills, whilst recreative activities, for example badminton, trampolining, etc., should be pursued outside normal school hours as recreative, leisure-time pursuits.

Only so can good results be achieved. Hard work and concentrated endeavour are the only means whereby our schools can produce results which will bear comparison with other countries. The pendulum has now swung too far, so that children are often allowed to choose which activity they want to do. This permissive approach to teaching – or rather 'occupying' – children during the P.E. lesson, can only result in poor attainments in comparison with actual potential of the pupils. Such gaps, in terms of educational attainment in the academic field between attainment age and chronological age would assuredly label any child as being retarded so many years. I think that this method of assessment should also apply to attainment in physical education.

No child in school, is permitted to choose whether or not he or she will do arithmetic or other academic subjects, and the same principle must apply to physical education. Children and adults need direction and children must learn to conform to certain disciplines. Every child, therefore, should take part in physical education as a vital part of his training and education.

Nowadays there is an increasing tendency to depart from the idea of 'a gymnasium for gymnastics' and the presence of gymnastic apparatus in the gymnasium is often considered a nuisance and a hindrance to the playing of minor games such as crab football. Such activities are a soft option for the teacher and are a poor substitute for properly prepared P.E. lessons. This type of activity does little to challenge pupils and cannot be considered to be part of a dynamic purposeful scheme of physical education. I have already mentioned trampolining but, excellent as this activity undoubtedly is for recreative gymnastics, I personally do not consider that to have one pupil performing on a trampoline whilst half a dozen others stand around safeguarding the performer is economic use of teaching time. So very often these days the trampoline is used as the sole activity for a P.E. lesson and when used in this way is the very antithesis of what a P.E. lesson should be. This apparatus may justifiably be used in a P.E. lesson when it is one of several pieces of apparatus used for group work.

To avoid giving a wrong impression I must add that I am as keen on athletics and outdoor activities as I am on gymnastics but nevertheless I am firmly of the opinion that gymnastics and gymnastic exercises are fundamental to all sports. It is incontrovertible that gymnastics, scientifically applied, provide for all-round development of the body. Olympic gymnastics, in particular, is a splendid means of practising brachial locomotion with its consequent excellent development of the upper body muscle groups. Games, on the other hand, tend to overdevelop lower girdle musculature and have a much less effect upon upper body development. Again, some sports and games lead to unequal development of muscle-groups on opposite sides of the body and even contribute a deformative effect. The game of hockey is an excellent example of the latter.

I do not offer the practice of gymnastics as the only answer to complete physical fitness and symmetrical development of the body. It does not, for example, develop the cardio-respiratory system to the same extent as running. What I *do* say is that gymnastics can be a sport for almost everyone, young and old alike, and according to its presentation it can provide interest, enjoyment, all round bodily development and stimulate a zest for living. The exercises can be graded to suit the personal attributes of the participant and I am convinced that if older people took part in such physical activity, they would add years to their life and stave off certain respiratory, muscular and circulatory disorders which often accompany middle and old age.

There is a tendency to regard gymnastics as the prerogative of the very young and then only of those, according to some pundits, 'with the skill and potential to perform'. This of course is absurd for, as I have already said, people of all ages can attain some measure of success and undoubtedly a great deal of enjoyment from such sport. It is regrettable that nowadays even P.E. men regard themselves as being too old at forty when really it is men of this age-group, with teaching and coaching experience, who are urgently needed to advise upon and develop our standards of performance in all sports. There is an over-emphasis on youth in the physical-education world, yet this quality is only transitory and young men become less physically able but older and wiser and much more efficient at their job. It is fallacious that a good performer should consequently be a good coach and teacher. The important thing is expertise and the ability to impart knowledge.

In his book *Psychology in Education* James B. Stroud states: 'Effectiveness of instruction is not determined so much by what the teacher does as what he leads the pupil to do.' I heartily concur with this assertion and I make a plea for the older, experienced teacher, who so often is overlooked for training and coaching positions, that he should be considered on his merits and not written off as being 'too old'. We are badly in need of such expertise and experience who, for example, would dream of writing off people like Sir Stanley Mathews? Yet this is happening frequently!

For very many years Olympic gymnastics was excluded from physical activities in British schools and colleges except for certain public schools which employed Army or Navy instructors. Thus few teachers outside the Services had the knowledge, training and experience to teach this type of gymnastics. During the past few years, however, steps have been taken by certain education authorities to reintroduce this activity into schools. Desirable and praiseworthy as this may be, dramatic results cannot be expected because of the shortage of qualified teachers and instructors capable of teaching this specialised work.

I hope then, that this book will remedy this deficiency and provide teachers with a sound basis on which to work. They will find that this type of gymnastics is not easy to master for it demands good basic strength especially of arms, shoulders and abdomen. Many heavy or overweight men will probably feel most embarrassed and inept when they first attempt the simple, basic exercises. My advice to them is 'persevere'. Master one exercise well before proceeding to attempt more difficult ones and you will gradually gain sufficient strength and skill to handle your body-weight really well.

The new and inexperienced teacher will probably find that the terminology and nomenclature somewhat difficult to comprehend. In this connection I have attempted a compromise by adapting the orthodox terminology to suit the purposes of this book. I have therefore dispensed with difficult descriptions as far as possible and substituted simple, self-explanatory descriptions instead. Even so, exercise description on Olympic apparatus is not easy and the reader will have to be patient and learn some of the starting positions first before attempting the exercises. Such time is well spent and later he may be able to give short descriptive names to certain exercises and thus evolve a terminology of his own.

Before proceeding to describe the various graded exercises I think it would be helpful to the reader if a list of starting positions was given, together with a brief description of each one. This will enable him to gain a knowledge of the language of Olympic gymnastics. Having learnt and practised the starting positions on the various pieces of apparatus he will then be able to add on simple movements and thus build up short sequence exercises of his own.

Such starting positions, therefore, may be performed as simple basic skills, e.g. *Toward End Standing (parallel bars), grasp bars and spring to Support position on the bars; dismount with legs swinging backwards.* Such practices during the early stages of learning and teaching would be the basic skills in a progressive system of learning and would provide

an essential foundation for progress to more difficult and am-
bitious feats.

The various starting positions are classified under appropriate headings, i.e. Standing, Sitting, Hanging, Resting, and
Balancing. These positions *must* be learnt.

STARTING POSITIONS FOR EXERCISES ON OLYMPIC GYMNASTIC APPARATUS

STANDING POSITIONS

Definition	*Description*
1. *Toward End Standing.* Parallel bars.	Standing outside the bars facing the end.
2. *Between Standing.* Parallel bars.	Standing between the bars facing along them. Variations of this: (*a*) at centre of bars. (*b*) at end of bars facing in. (*c*) at end of bars facing out.
3. *Toward Outside Standing.* Parallel bars.	Standing outside the bars facing the side of the appar-atus. (*a*) at centre of bars. (*b*) to left or right of centre.
4. *Toward Side Standing.* Parallel bars.	Standing outside the bars with side of body towards them.
5. *Toward Inside Standing.* Parallel bars.	Standing between the bars with shoulders parallel with the long axis of the bar.
6. *Toward Back Standing.*	Standing with back to appa-ratus.

SITTING POSITIONS

Definition	*Description*
1. *Astride Sitting.* Parallel bars, horizontal bar, pommel horse.	Sitting astride the apparatus facing along the long axis. Additional details may be added, e.g. legs bent or legs straight.

2. *Sitting (Fig.* 1).
Parallel bar, horizontal bar, horse, etc.

Sitting on apparatus with shoulders parallel with the long axis. Legs may be bent or straight, and may be *between* the bars, on the parallel bars, or outside. The sitting position may be qualified accordingly, e.g. sitting legs between bars – bent (parallel bars).

3. *Side Sitting (Fig.* 2).
Parallel bars, horizontal bar, horse, etc.

Sitting on apparatus with shoulders at right angles to the long axis. The pupil sits on one thigh with leg bent whilst the other leg hangs straight down.

4. *Front or Forward Astride Sitting (Fig.* 3).
Parallel bars, horizontal bar, pommel horse.

Sitting astride the apparatus with shoulders parallel with the long axis.

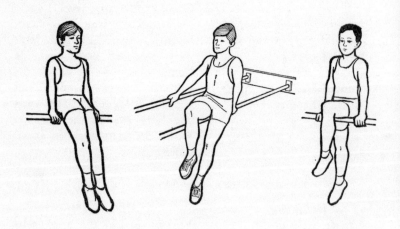

FIG. 1. Sitting: shoulders in line with long axis of apparatus: FIG. 2. Outside side sitting, right knee bent: FIG. 3. Front/forward astride sitting: starting position for backward mill-circle etc. Shoulders in line with bar. Weight partly borne by arms.

HANGING POSITIONS

Definition	*Description*
1. *Overgrasp Hang (Fig. 4).* Beam, horizontal bar, rings.	Suspended from apparatus by the straight arms with hands in pronation, i.e. backs of hands towards face. The body hangs straight down, hip, knee and ankle joints extended and toes pointed.
2. *Undergrasp Hang (Fig. 5).*	As described for 1 above but with hands in supination, i.e. palms of hands towards face.

FIG. 4. Overgrasp hang: FIG. 5. Undergrasp hang.

3. *Bent-Arm Hang.*	From overgrasp or undergrasp hang the arms are flexed so that the head is held level with or a little above bar level.
4. *Upper-Arm Hang (Fig. 6).* Parallel bars.	The extended body hangs supported by the upper arms resting on the bars, hands grasping the bars in front, elbows partly flexed.
5. *Inverted Hang.* Parallel bars, horizontal bar, rings and ropes.	The body suspended by the hands and with the extended body inverted, i.e. head downwards legs overhead.

6. *Inward-Grasp Hang.*
   Rings, ropes and parallel bars.

The body suspended from apparatus with palms of hands turned inwards as in rope climbing.

7. *Combined-Grasp Hang.* (*Fig. 7*).

Suspended from a horizontal bar or beam with one hand in undergrasp and the other in overgrasp.

FIG. 6. Upper arm hang: FIG. 7. Combined grasp hang.

RESTING POSITIONS

Definition	*Description*
1. *Front Rest or Support* (Balance Support). Parallel bars, horizontal bar, beam.	The body-weight is borne wholly by the straight arms with the front of the thighs resting against the apparatus.
2. *Back Rest.*	As for the previous position but with the backs of the thighs resting against the apparatus.
3. *Astride Rest.* Parallel bars, horizontal bar, beam.	Body weight borne by the straight arms and legs astride the apparatus – facing along the long axis.

4. *Front Astride Rest.*
   Parallel bars, horizontal bar, beam.

As for Front Rest, opposite, but with legs astride the apparatus.

5. *Front Support Thigh Rest.*
   e.g. across the parallel bars.

The body-weight is borne equally between the arms, hands grasping one bar and the thighs resting on the other.

6. *Front Support Rest (Fig.* 8) (Front Support).
   Parallel bars.

The extended body, face downwards, is supported by straight arms and the toes.

7. *Between Rest Support* (*Fig.* 9).
   Parallel bars.

The body-weight is supported by the straight arms, one hand on each bar, body completely extended and toes pointed. Thumbs around bar.

8. *Between Rest, Half Lever.*

From the rest position the legs are raised forward, toes well pointed, heels about one foot above the level of the bars.

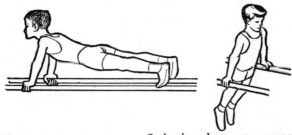

FIG. 8. Front support: FIG. 9. Swinging between support/rest position on parallel bars. *Note* thumbs around bar.

BALANCES

Definition	*Description*
1. *Double-Shoulder Balance* (*Fig.* 10). Parallel bars.	From Support position on bars swing up to a short-arm balance, i.e. body inverted and arms fully bent, and place the upper arms on the bars.

2. *Single-Shoulder Balance.* Parallel bars.

3. *Across-Shoulder Balance.* Parallel bars.

As for 1 (page 21) but with only one arm resting on the bar. Facing side of bars, grasp near bar with under-grasp and mount to Balance-Support. Allow the body to rotate forwards and place the shoulders on further bar; keep the arms strongly flexed and mount to shoulder-balance on bar.

4. *Short- or Bent-Arm Balance (Fig. 11).* Parallel bars, horizontal bar, pommel horse.

The inverted body is supported by the fully flexed arms, shoulders clear of the bars/apparatus.

5. *Hand Balance (Fig. 12).* Parallel bars, horizontal bar.

The inverted, extended body is supported by straight arms.

6. *Single-Hand Balance.* Parallel bars, etc.

The inverted, extended body is supported by one straight arm only.

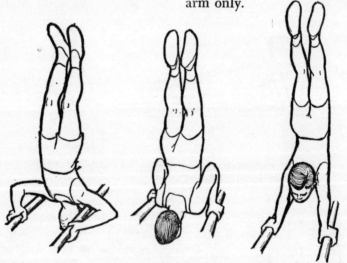

FIG. 10. Shoulder balance. *Note* elbows pointing sideways:
FIG. 11. Short arm balance. *Note* fully flexed arms close to sides:
FIG. 12. Long arm balance (hand stand). *Note* locked shoulders – straight arms, head pressed back.

TWO

PROGRESSIVE EXERCISES

When you have made a study of the foregoing starting positions and have mastered the terminology, go on to practise the following progressive skills on the different pieces of apparatus. The exercises described here are not very difficult or comprehensive in scope but they will provide a basic course on Olympic gymnastics which can be taught in schools and which should be well within the abilities of both masters and pupils.

Here are some simple parallel bar exercises:

(A) TRAVELLING MOVEMENTS

In these the pupil travels from one end of the bars to the other by various means, using his arms only or arms and legs together, or perhaps rolling along the bars. They may be considered introductory exercises which serve to get the pupil used to taking his body weight solely on his arms, thereby conditioning him for the more strenuous exercises to follow.

1. STARTING POSITION: *Standing facing the ends of the bars at arm's length away.* (Toward End Standing.)

Grasp the ends of the bars and mount to support position at the same time swinging the straight legs forward to place a leg on each bar (astride sitting). Now, keeping the legs straight and toes well pointed, push away with both hands. As the trunk moves forward, extend the hips, pivoting on the insides of the thighs, and swing the arms forward to regrasp the bars in front. Without pause, half flex both arms to bring the trunk over the hands and swing the straight legs up behind to meet in the mid-line. Swing down between bars and allow the legs to swing well up in front. Part the legs and place one leg over each bar to assume the original astride sitting position. Repeat the whole movement along the length of the bars and dismount by allowing the legs to swing well up in advance of the body and then pushing away with the arms as the legs arc downwards – similar to an undershoot dismount on the horizontal bar. The landing must be made on the balls of the feet with ankle, knee and hip joints bending slightly to absorb the landing shock.

SHORT DESCRIPTION OF EXERCISE: *Astride travel on bars. Plate* 1, facing page 32, shows astride sitting.

2. *Starting position: Toward End Standing.*
Grasp the bars and spring to support position. Now practise a body-swing between the bars keeping the legs straight and swinging freely from the shoulders. Swing both legs forward on to the left bar, at the same time flexing the hips and assuming a side sitting position on the bar, right knee bent and left leg stretched straight down. This position is known as outside side sitting; the shoulders are facing square to the front and the performer is therefore looking along the length of the bars.

Next, change the hand grasp from rear to front, at the same time swinging the trunk forward and semi-flexing the arms. As this movement occurs, swing the legs up behind and then downwards – forwards between the bars. At the end of the swing place both legs over and on to the right bar to take up the outside side sitting position again. Repeat the whole movement along the length of the bars and, when the end of the bars is reached, dismount by:

(i)   From the outside side sitting position at the end of the bars, by swinging both legs forward, outside the bars, and at the same time pushing away with both hands from their rear position on the bars.

(ii) By grasping the ends of the bars in front and then swinging the legs up behind and downwards between the bars. Check the leg swing in front as the feet reach chest height and then shoot them down towards the floor. At the same time push away vigorously with the arms and land with back towards the ends of the bars.

(iii) From side sitting, grasp ends of bars in front and lean back to the full extent of the arms. The body should now be in a jack-knife position – legs straight and toes well pointed. Now, with a strong heave from the arms,

rock the hips up to a position above the hands and perform an overswing dismount from the end of the bars.
This is a difficult movement and assistance from a supporter will be needed in the learning stages.

SHORT DESCRIPTION OF EXERCISE: *Progressive side sitting
with Intermediate body-swing – optional dismount.*

3. *Starting Position: Toward End Standing.*
Grasp the bars and spring to a support position. Now
straight-arm walk along the bars, transferring body-weight
from one arm to the other as the step forward is made. Take
short steps at first and dismount by bending arms and placing feet on the base.

SHORT DESCRIPTION OF EXERCISE: *Support position.
Straight-arm walk along bars.*

4. *Starting position: Toward End Standing.*
Grasp bars and spring to support position. Straight-arm
walk along bars with alternate knee raising. As the hand shift
is made the knee on the opposite side is raised high and the
whole progression along the bars is done rhythmically and
without pause.

SHORT DESCRIPTION OF EXERCISE: *Straight-arm walk along
bars with alternate high knee raising.*

5. *Starting position: Toward End Standing.*
Grasp bars and spring to support position. Commence a
body-swing between the bars by first swinging the legs forward and then allowing them to swing backwards. Increase
the momentum and as the feet reach their highest point in
front, hop forwards on the hands a few inches. Again, when
the feet reach their high point behind hop backwards a few
inches. Now try to hop progressively along the bars, hopping
forward each time the feet reach their high point in front
and rear.

SHORT DESCRIPTION OF EXERCISE: *Swing-hopping forward
along the bars.*

6. *Starting position: Toward End Standing.*
Grasp the bars and vault to sit astride them (astride sit-

ting). Now grasp bars a little way in front – about 9 inches –
and lean well back with straight arms. From here, heave
strongly with the arms and, rocking the seat upwards and forwards with knees tucked well up, round the back and
commence a forward-roll, moving the elbows outwards and
placing the upper arms on the bars. Continue the roll and as
the hips approach the bar again, part the legs ready to
place them astride the bars. As the hips move downwards the
hand-grasp is released and the tucked up, compact body rolls
on the upper arms; the arms are swung forward to grasp the
bars in front as the head and trunk swing upwards and forwards to reach the original starting position.

SHORT DESCRIPTION OF EXERCISE: *Astride sitting forward
grasp. Forward straddle-roll along bars. (See Fig. 13.)*

Teaching points: The elbows must be kept well out from
the sides in order to avoid slipping down between the bars.
A supporter may assist the movement by giving the pupil
some 'lift' from *beneath* the bars. It must be noted that the
supporter should never place his arm across the bars when
spotting any exercise because of the danger of a pupil dropping on to his arm and occasioning some injury. Throughout
the roll the pupil must remain either in a piked or tuck position and the roll must continue without pause. Should he
open out during the roll, by extending his hips, he will not
complete the movement but will lie spreadeagled on the
bars. Ideally the legs should be kept straight throughout, as
the weight of the dropping legs with the body in a piked

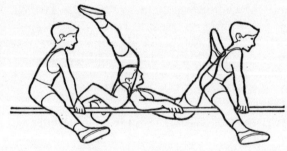

FIG. 13. Forward straddle roll along bars. *Note* straight legs,
pointed toes. Downward swing of straight legs assists in forward
rotation of trunk.

position assists the forward-upward rotation of the head and trunk.

(B) SWINGING AND TURNING MOVEMENTS PERFORMED FROM SUPPORT POSITION ON THE BARS

1. *Starting position: Between Standing at end of bars facing out.*

Grasp bars and spring to support position. Swing between bars and when legs are well up behind, part them and place a foot on each bar – front support position. Either the toes or the inside of the feet may be placed on the bar and from this position the right leg is swung down between the bars and then vigorously upwards to be joined by the left leg at peak height after a thrust away from the bar. A face-vault is then performed over the left bar and as the body passes over, the right hand is transferred to the left bar and the left hand is brought quickly away and swung sideways-upwards following a push-away from the bar. The landing is made in side standing – side of body towards apparatus – with the right hand grasping the bar.

FIG. 14. Face vault dismount to side standing. *Note* quick transfer of left hand to right bar.

SHORT DESCRIPTION OF EXERCISE: *Front support on bars; single-leg swinging between bars and face-vault dismount over left or right bar.*

Fig. 14. Shows face-vault right to finish in side standing.

2. *Starting position: Support position at centre of bars.*

Body-swing between bars, swinging freely from the shoulders, then with legs well up in front, dismount by swinging them over the left bar. At the same time transfer the right hand from the right to the left bar, releasing the grasp of the left hand and swinging the arm sideways upwards to impart 'lift'. The landing is made in side standing with near hand grasping the bar.

SHORT DESCRIPTION OF EXERCISE: *From support position between the bars: body-swing and dismount by rear-vault over the left bar.*

Fig. 15 A. Shows rear-vault dismount.

Fig. 15 B. Shows flight and hand transference.

Fig. 15 C. Shows landing in side standing.

Teaching points: Instruct the pupil to swing the straight legs well up in front so that the body is in a jack-knife posi-

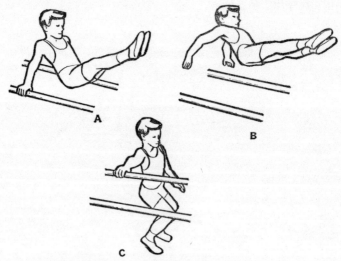

FIG. 15. (*a*) Showing rear vault dismount. *Note* straight legs and pointed toes; (*b*) Showing flight and hand transference; (*c*) Showing landing in side standing grasp.

tion as it passes over the bar. The right hand must be brought quickly across as the vault is made, in order to support the body-weight. Do not bend the arms during weight transference. The left hand must be brought quickly away from the bar and swung vigorously sideways-upwards in order to offset 'dropping' or lateral rotation of the body. When supporting for this exercise the supporter should stand on the side of the bars towards which the vault is being made and should be behind the performer. As the performer clears the bar the supporter may give some support just under the armpits and guide the performer to a safe landing.

3. *Starting position: Support position at centre of bars.*
Body-swing between bars with increasing height until the legs are well above bar level behind. As the feet reach peak height, push away strongly with the right arm and perform a face-vault over the left bar at the same time quickly transferring the right hand to the left bar to support the body weight as the left arm is swung sideways-upwards. The landing is made in side standing with the right hand grasping the right bar.

SHORT DESCRIPTION OF EXERCISE: *Support position between bars; body-swing and face-vault over left bar.*

Teaching points: Practise a free shoulder swing so that the extended body assumes a horizontal position when the legs are behind, i.e. on the backward swing. Do not allow the legs to swing too high in front but check the downwards-forwards swing each time by tightening arm and shoulder muscles. It will be found that a slight bending of the arms on the back swing, followed by a straightening of the arms will facilitate attaining leg elevation behind. All segments of the body should be in line with head slightly pressed back, toes well pointed and arms perfectly straight as the bar clearance is made.

4. *Starting position: Between Standing. Grasp bars and spring to Support position.*
Swing between bars and when the legs are forward swing them over and on to the left bar to assume a side sitting position on that bar, hands grasping the bar behind. Keep the

legs straight and, taking most of the body weight on to the left arm, push away with the right arm and make a quarter-left body-turn, transferring the grasp of the right hand to the left bar. In the position thus reached most of the body weight is borne by the arms, with the backs of the thighs resting against the bar – the hips slightly flexed (back support). Dismount by swinging the legs forward, at the same time pushing away with both arms. Land with back towards apparatus.

SHORT DESCRIPTION: *Dismount from side sitting with a quarter-left body-turn, forward leg swing and arm thrust-away.*

5. *Starting position: Between Standing at centre of bars.*

Grasp bars and spring to support position. Now keeping the arms perfectly straight push away with the right arm to transfer the body-weight on to the left arm. At the same time make a quarter-left body-turn and transfer the grasp of the right hand to the left bar. The position reached is front support or balance support and the body leans slightly forwards, arms straight and with no bend at the hips. A further body turn is now made to the left with the weight being transferred to the right arm as the turn is made, to support position on both bars. Continue the exercise until a complete turn has been made and the original starting position is reached.

SHORT DESCRIPTION: *From between standing to support position; continuous quarter-left turns between bars.*

Teaching points: With practice the turns may be performed rhythmically and without pause. The object of the exercise is to develop arm and shoulder strength and ability to transfer body-weight from one arm to the other – so necessary in all parallel bar work.

6. *Starting position: Support position at centre of bars.*

Swing between bars and when on a forward swing, as the feet reach maximum height in front, release the hand grasp, simultaneously, and make a quick and snappy body-twist – hips first, then the trunk – to achieve a half-left turn; regrasp the bars quickly and continue swinging between the bars.

SHORT DESCRIPTION OF EXERCISE: *Support at centre of bars; body-swing and forward swinging half-left body-turn with hand release and re-grasp after turn.*

Teaching points: do not swing too high at first and make tentative turns to finish standing on base of bars. This may well be practised initially at the end of the bars facing out so that a complete swinging half-left/right body-turn may be made before landing on the floor. With increasing confidence in his ability the pupil may later attempt the complete movement from support position at centre of bars.

(C) LEG CIRCLING MOVEMENTS

These exercises are more difficult to perform than those in the previous sections, and good timing is essential for skilful performance. In addition, weight transference from one arm to the other must be practised so that when the right leg is circled, body-weight is taken by the left arm and vice-versa. These points must be borne in mind when practising the following exercises.

1. *Starting position: Between Standing at centre of bars. Grasp bars and spring to Support position.*

Body-swing and, at the end of a back-swing, sharply flex the hips to a pike position, i.e. the hips will rise and the legs swing forward. As the forward-swing ensues, transfer the body-weight on to the left arm, push-away with the right arm and release the hand grasp momentarily for the right leg to circle forward over the right bar. Re-grasp with the right hand as both legs meet at centre, and continue body-swing between bars. Repeat the exercise to the opposite side.

SHORT DESCRIPTION: *Support position at centre of bars; body-swing and at end of back-swing pike and forward (left) circle of right leg over right bar.*

2. *Starting position: Between Standing at centre of bars.*

Grasp bars and spring to support position, continuing straight away into a body-swing. At the end of a back swing flex hips and, transferring weight on to the left arm, circle both legs forward over the right bar, releasing the right hand grasp for the legs to pass and re-grasping afterwards.

SHORT DESCRIPTION OF EXERCISE: *Support at centre of bars; body-swing between bars and forward circle both legs over right bar at end of back swing.* See *Figs.* 16a b, c and d.

Teaching points: As a lead up to this difficult exercise try circling both legs forward to a side sitting position on the right bar – no weight transference will be necessary for this exercise. Later, attempt the complete movement but remember to lean the body-weight well over to the opposite side, keeping the supporting arm straight. Later on, the double

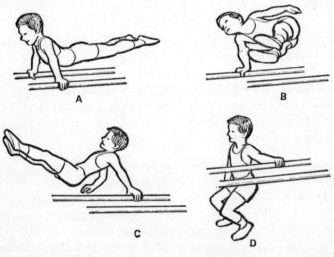

FIG. 16. (*a*) Swinging in support position. Swing loosely from shoulders; (*b*) Forward circle. Both legs over left bar. *Note* weight transfer to right arm; (*c*) Bar clearance completed; (*d*) Movement completed to finish in side standing, left hand grasping bar.

leg circle may be attempted to clear both bars in a pike position – legs well elevated. This exercise is known as a swinging rear-vault over both bars to finish in a side standing position – a most difficult exercise.

3. *Starting position: Toward End Standing.*

Grasp bars and spring to support position on bars and descend immediately. Practise this movement many times, keeping the arms straight, and finally repeat the movement at the

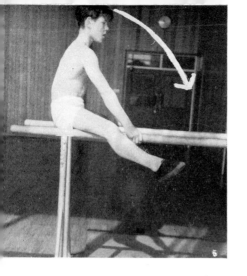

PLATE 1. Astride sitting

PLATE 2. Inward circle of both legs over right bar

PLATE 3. Showing support for inward circle of legs

PLATE 4. Astride inward circle of both legs to rest. Note support

PLATE 5. Reverse astride dismount at end of bars

PLATE 6. Showing spotter intent as pupil dismounts

same time circling the right leg inwards over the end of the right bar, removing the grasp of the right hand for the leg to pass. Finish in support position and immediately descend. Repeat the whole movement several times rhythmically and then repeat to the opposite side.

SHORT DESCRIPTION OF EXERCISE: *Toward end standing-grasp: spring to support position with single leg circling inwards over end of bar.*

Teaching points: Do not try to stay in support position at first but descend immediately. When one side has been mastered, attempt the movement to the opposite side and then with alternate legs. Later, practise to stay up in the support position but remember to transfer body-weight on to the opposite arm as the leg circle is made.

4. *Starting position: Toward End Standing.*

Grasp the ends of the bars and with a spring and strong downward pressure of the almost straight arms, left circle both legs inwards over the end of the right bar, removing the grasp of the right hand for the legs to pass. Continue the leg circle by allowing the legs to swing downwards between the bars and as the legs commence to swing backwards, dismount by pushing away with both arms to finish in the original starting position. See *Plate 2* (facing page 32), showing inward circle of both legs over right bar.

SHORT DESCRIPTION OF EXERCISE: *Toward end standing-inward grasp: spring to support at the same time circling both legs together, inwards over the right bar. Descend as legs swing back.*

Teaching points: This is not an easy movement and it is best first to spring to support position and circle the legs over the end of the bar to arrive in a side sitting position on the right bar. Next, with hands grasping the bar behind, swing both legs forwards-upwards and back down between the bars dismounting, as the legs swing back. This is a very useful intermediate stage and after the complete leg circle has been mastered, without stopping in side sitting, then a double leg circle inwards should be attempted stopping in a support position.

When attempting such circles it is well to have a supporter

standing behind the pupil and, by grasping his waist or the waistband of his trousers/shorts, imparting some much needed 'lift' as the pupil attempts the movement. The method of support is clearly shown in *Plate 3* (facing page 32), showing method of support for inward circle of legs over right bar to support.

5. *Starting position: Toward End Standing.*

Grasp bars, spring to support position and immediately dismount by pushing away with the arms. Repeat this movement several times keeping the arms straight so that the body rides away from the bars on the dismount. Finally, spring to support, at the same time swinging both legs together to just above bar height; dismount, as before, by riding away on straight arms and at the same time circling the right leg outwards over the end of the right bar, releasing the grasp of the right hand for the leg to pass. Re-grasp the bar after the leg clearance and land, still grasping the bars, at full arm's length away.

SHORT DESCRIPTION OF EXERCISE: *Toward end Standing: spring to support, swing legs to above bar height and dismount with right leg circling outwards over the right bar.*

Teaching points: Remember to transfer the weight on to the left arm as the circle is made. Keep the supporting arm straight all the time. Support, as described, must be provided in the learning stages.

6. *Starting position: Toward End Standing.*

The previous exercise may be done with both legs circling together outwards over the end of the bar. This is a much more difficult movement and should be first practised by circling both legs outwards to assume a side sitting position on the right bar – if the circle is being made to the right side. Later, the whole movement may be attempted with a supporter supporting at the waist and guiding the movement. If sufficient 'lift' is not given during the learning process the pupil may strike the outside of his left thigh on the bar and this can be very painful. The supporter must watch for this and must give sufficient 'lift' to ensure that the pupil does clear the bar.

SHORT DESCRIPTION OF EXERCISE: *Toward end standing: spring to support and dismount immediately with both legs circling outwards over the right bar.*

7. *Starting position: Toward End Standing.*

Grasp both bars and with a spring mount to sit astride the bars, removing the grasp of both hands simultaneously for the legs to pass and then quickly re-grasping behind. Repeat this movement several times with more vigour and pressing down very strongly with the arms. It will be found that the legs can be swung clear over the ends of the bars to meet in the centre line and the movement completed in support position.

SHORT DESCRIPTION OF EXERCISE: *Toward end standing: grasp bars and, with a spring, astride inward circle of both legs over ends of bars to finish in support position.* See *Plate 4* (facing page 33), showing astride inward circle of legs to rest. Note support.

Teaching points: To ensure success with this skill, stand three or four paces away from the end of the bars, then walk smartly towards them. Without pause, grasp the ends of the bars and by pressing downwards with the arms, coinciding with a vigorous spring, attempt a straddle cut inwards over the end of the bars keeping the legs quite straight. Land in astride sitting on the bars and as the thighs contact the bars the hands should be grasping the bars behind. Let the thighs bounce on the bars and then, from the rebound, swing both legs up and back down between the bars, continuing the leg swing and dismounting to return to the original starting position. After several tries at this the complete movement should be attempted with a supporter grasping the waist-band of the pupil's shorts centrally behind and walking quickly forward with the pupil as he makes his approach. By giving the pupil 'lift' the supporter can ensure that the pupil completes the movement safely and successfully.

8. *Starting position: Toward End Standing.*

Grasp bars and spring to support position, at the same time swinging the legs forwards-upwards between the bars and parting them to sit astride. Repeat the movement with more speed but instead of parting the legs and finishing sitting astride the bars, the arms push strongly away and the legs swing back clear astride the bars. Finish in a standing position facing the end of the bars.

SHORT DESCRIPTION OF EXERCISE: *Toward end standing: grasp bars, spring to support and immediately perform a reverse astride dismount.* See *Plate* 5, facing page 33, reverse astride dismount over end of bars.

Teaching points: This movement demands daring and confidence. Support must be provided during the learning stages for there is always the danger that if the thighs lock the hands on the bars, because the hands are not removed quickly enough, the pupil may pivot over backwards and a very dangerous situation arise. It must be stressed that when the legs are at their high point in the support position and are being circled outwards over the ends of the bars, then the arms must thrust-away very strongly in order to keep the trunk upright and to offset a tendency to backward rotation. The following stages will be found useful as leading up exercises:

(a) Practice circling outwards with single legs first as previously described.

(b) Next, practise walking briskly towards the bars, grasping them and mounting to sit astride them, bringing the legs forcibly backwards to contact the hands. A supporter must stand behind in case the pupil loses balance and pivots over backwards.

(c) Finally, attempt the complete movement from a toward end standing position, with a supporter giving assistance as already described. See *Plate* 6, facing page 33, showing spotter intent as pupil dismounts.

9. *Starting position: Between Standing at end of bars facing out.*

Grasp bars and mount to support position. Body-swing between bars and at the end of a backward-swing, as the forward swing ensues, swing the right leg forward over the right bar (left circle right leg over right bar) releasing the grasp of the right hand for the leg to pass, and dismount with a quarter-left body-turn pivoting on the straight left arm and retaining the hand grasp until a landing is made.

SHORT DESCRIPTION OF EXERCISE: *Support position at end of bars facing out; swinging forward astride dismount over right bar with a quarter-left turn.*

Teaching points: Transfer the body-weight on to the left arm as the right leg circles the bar. As the leg circle is commenced, the hips must be sharply flexed so that the hips are raised and there is then no danger of the crutch coming into painful contact with the bar. The supporting left arm must be kept straight throughout so that the performer rides outwards on it and thus lands a full arm's length from the end of the bar.

10. *Starting position: Support at end of bars facing out.*

This exercise is similar to the preceding one except that from a free body-swing the legs are parted at the high point of the back-swing; then following a quick hip flexion, the legs are swung forward over the ends of the bars to perform an astride dismount. See *Plate* 7, facing page 48, showing forward astride dismount over ends of bars.

SHORT DESCRIPTION OF EXERCISE: *Support at end of bars facing out; swinging forward astride dismount over ends of bars.*

Teaching points: As the legs are parted and brought forward astride the bars, the arms must thrust strongly away in order to project the body-weight upwards-forwards thus ensuring leg clearance and avoiding the danger of the thighs locking the hands on to the bars. This sometimes happens with timid learners and there is then the possibility of the pupil rotating helplessly forwards and landing on his head. It is important therefore that a supporter should be present, facing him, and as the pupil attempts the cut-off, the supporter grasps the pupil's upper arms and steps backwards as he comes forward; at the same time he is able to 'lift' and 'pull' thus ensuring that the pupil does clear the ends of the bars. After several such tries the pupil should soon accomplish the skill unaided.

38   OLYMPIC GYMNASTICS FOR SCHOOLS

(D) UNCLASSIFIED MISCELLANEOUS SKILLS

1. *Starting position: Toward Outside Standing facing centre of bars.*

Grasp the near bar with overgrasp-arms at full stretch and hands shoulder-width apart. With a spring and a heave, mount to front support thigh rest on near bar and immediately transfer the hands, one at a time, to grasp the far bar. The body-weight will now be borne equally by the arms and thighs, the body being nicely extended, toes pointed and head pressed back (chin in). From this position cast-away by pushing away strongly with both arms, coinciding with a backwards-upwards swing of the legs, and perform a shoot-away dismount to land facing the bars with both hands grasping the near bar. Quarter left or right turns may be added as the dismount is made so that a landing is made in side standing position to the bars. *Plate* 8, facing page 48, shows front support thigh rest.

SHORT DESCRIPTION OF EXERCISE: *Toward outside standing facing centre of bars; overgrasp-mount to front support thigh rest across bars – grasping furthest bar – cast-away dismount backwards to finish facing bars.*

Teaching points: Remember to keep weight well over arms, and swing legs well up when casting away – thrust vigorously with the arms. When adding a quarter left/right turn, push away first with the arm on the side towards which the turn is being made; then swing this arm sideways-outwards to turn the trunk around. Bar clearance is then assured by thrusting away strongly with the opposite arm as the turn is made.

2. *Starting position: Toward Outside Standing facing centre of bars.*

Grasp bars and mount to front support thigh rest, as in previous exercise. Now bounce the thighs up and down several times on the bar checking the descent each time by tightening the arm and shoulder muscles. Finally, quickly flex the hips and knees (tuck knees up towards the chest) and bring the feet over the bar, immediately extending knee and hip joints to land between the bars. The grasp of the far bar is retained throughout.

SHORT DESCRIPTION OF EXERCISE: *Front support thigh rest across bars. Thigh bounce followed by a through-vault to land standing between the bars.*

Teaching points: Practise first to bounce thighs and elevate the seat to get both feet together on to the bar (crouch position on bar) transferring more weight on to the hands as this is done. A supporter may assist by standing outside the bars facing the performer and, by grasping the pupil's upper arm with one hand and placing his other hand on the pupil's chest, giving some 'lift' as the attempt is made.

3. *Starting position: As for the previous exercise.*

This exercise is an advance on the previous one and the pupil after a preliminary thigh bounce performs a through-vault over both bars to land with his back towards them.

SHORT DESCRIPTION OF EXERCISE: *Front support thigh rest. Through-vault over bars to land standing with back to bars.*

Teaching points: The movement should be preceded by a thigh bounce to provide some impetus and the vault should immediately follow-on without hesitation. At the same time the arms must execute a vigorous pull-push action in order to provide forward movement. Support must be provided by an assistant standing side-on near the pupil's head. He then grasps the pupil's upper arm with his outside hand whilst the near arm is elevated, ready to place the hand behind the pupil's seat as he attempts the movement, in order to give 'lift' and forward impetus. The danger is that the pupil may catch his feet on the bar as he vaults and it is therefore essential that the supporter must be able to pull the pupil forward with one hand whilst with the other he can lift and push. When, with increasing confidence, the pupil can attempt the vault unaided, the assistant merely 'spots' the movement, standing facing the pupil and renders assistance only if necessary. This is best done by placing the upraised hands in proximity to the pupil's chest as he comes over and stepping backwards with him as he lands.

4. *Starting position: Toward Outside Standing facing centre of bars.*

Grasp near bar with combined grasp, i.e. one hand in undergrasp and the other in overgrasp. In this case the left hand is in undergrasp and the other in overgrasp. With a spring and a powerful pull-push of both arms, flank-vault left over near bar with quarter-left turn as the legs reach their high point. The right hand then grasps the right bar as the turn is made and the pupil now swings between the bars in support position. As the legs swing forwards-upwards a rear-vault left is made in front of the left hand..

SHORT DESCRIPTION OF EXERCISE: *Toward outside standing facing centre of bars – combined grasp, left hand under and right hand over. Flank-vault right over near bar with a quarter-left turn to swinging support position on both bars and rear-vault left in front of left hand.*

Teaching points: First practise to vault over the near bar and land standing between the bars. Next, repeat the movement but adding a quarter-left turn to land on the base of the bars facing towards the end. The next stage is to attempt the movement with the turn to stay up in the support position on the bars. Later still, continue with the forward swing after reaching the support position and finish in side sitting on the left bar in front of the hands. It is then but a short step to the final movement.

5. *Starting position: Toward Outside standing facing centre of bars.*

Grasp the near bar with overgrasp and spring with a quarter-left turn to assume a side sitting position on the near bar (sitting on the right thigh, left leg extended straight down). As the spring is made the right hand is transferred to the far bar. Now, with hands grasping the bar behind, swing both legs well up in front and over on to the opposite bar to assume a side sitting position on that bar. Next dismount by swinging both legs forwards-upwards and then downwards, coinciding with a strong push-away from the arms. As the dismount is made the left hand is transferred to the right bar and the landing is made in side standing with left hand grasping the left bar.

SHORT DESCRIPTION OF EXERCISE: *Toward outside standing facing the centre of the bars. Overgrasp and mount to side sitting on near bar, facing left. Behind-grasp and swing legs over and on to opposite bar to side sitting position. Dismount with legs swinging forwards to finish in side standing.*

6. *Starting position: Toward Outside Standing facing centre of bars.*

Overgrasp-hands shoulder-width apart and mount to side sitting on near bar facing left. Grasp behind and swing legs up and clean over the opposite bar to land in side standing position. As the body passes over the far bar the left hand is quickly transferred to the right bar and the right hand is quickly removed and swung sideways-upwards to offset lateral rotation.

SHORT DESCRIPTION OF EXERCISE: *From side sitting on near bar, rear-vault over far bar to land in side standing.*

7. *Starting position: Toward Outside Standing facing centre of bars.*

Grasp bars and mount with quarter-right turn to side sitting on near bar. Grasp bars behind, swing legs up in front and body swing between bars. Swing straight legs well up in front and rear-vault left with a quarter-right turn to finish facing the bars grasping the near bar with both hands in overgrasp.

SHORT DESCRIPTION OF EXERCISE: *Toward outside standing at centre of bars: Mount to side sitting on near bar facing right. Swing legs up in front and body-swing between bars. Rear-vault left with a quarter-right turn. Finish facing bars.*

Teaching points: When performing rear-vault with turns, the body-turn is initiated by the arms. In the case of a rear-vault left, the right hand thrusts strongly against the right bar before the hand is quickly transferred to the left bar whilst the left arm is swung vigorously right at the same time as the legs swing downwards-inwards towards the bars. The legs should be well elevated before being swung down for if they just scrape over the bars it is not then possible to secure a good, fast turn. Later, half- or three-quarter turns may be added to the rear-vault dismount.

8. *Starting position: Toward Outside Standing facing centre of bars.*

The exercise, up to the body-swing between bars is as for the previous exercise but on a backward swing as the extended body rises parallel with the bars a face-vault left/ right is performed to finish in side standing with the near hand grasping the near bar.

SHORT DESCRIPTION OF EXERCISE: *Toward outside standing facing centre of bars. Spring, with a quarter-left turn to side sitting on near bar. Grasp bar behind and swing legs up and down between bars. On a backward swing of legs, face-vault left/right and dismount to finish in side standing.*

Teaching points: In both the face- and rear-vaults the hand shift must be quickly and deftly made so that the point of support is directly under the body as it passes over the bar. In the face-vault the body should be nicely extended – no visible kinks – arms straight and head pressed back (chin in). Little assistance is required with these vaults but when they are being learnt it is well to have a spotter nearby.

9. *Starting position: Toward Outside Standing facing centre of bars.*

Grasp near bar with overgrasp – hands shoulder-width apart – and spring with a quarter-right turn to side sitting on near bar. Now transfer the grasp of the left hand to the far bar and extend the right arm well behind but not grasping the bar. From this position swing the right arm vigorously over to grasp the far bar, at the same time vigorously extending the hips and swinging the right leg upwards-forwards – quickly followed by the left leg – to perform a flank-vault over the far bar. During the vault the extended body should be horizontal and parallel with the bars. As the legs attain maximum height the right arm is placed alongside the body; the hips are brought up and the head thrown over to the left to get all segments of the body in line. For a brief moment the body is parallel with the bar and the supporting arm perpendicular to it. A landing is made with the back towards the bars.

SHORT DESCRIPTION OF EXERCISE: *Toward outside standing facing centre of bars. Grasp bars and with a quarter-right turn mount to outside side sitting on near bar. Hands be-hind, grasp. Flank-vault over far bar to finish standing with back to bars.* See *Fig.* 17, showing outside side sitting to flank-vault dismount.

10. *Starting position: Toward Outside Standing facing centre of bars.*

Undergrasp-hands shoulder-width apart and spring to bal-ance support on near bar, keeping body completely extended, toes pointed and head pressed back. Now, keeping the arms

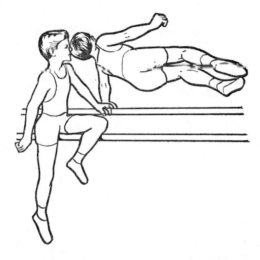

FIG. 17. Outside side sitting to flank vault dismount. *Note* swing over of right arm and weight supported on vertical left arm.

straight, pivot forward on hands and front of thighs to lie across the bars with shoulders resting on the far bar and head overhanging it. The arms must now be slightly flexed in order to prevent the shoulders slipping forward off the bar. Then, by raising the seat and sliding the legs on the bar, rotate the seat forwards until it is over the shoulders and then tuck the legs up to attain a tuck shoulder balance on the bar. Later, extend the hips and legs slowly so that a shoulder balance proper is achieved. The return from the balance may be made in either of two ways (*a*) along the

same path in reverse, i.e. tucking up from the extended position and returning to lie across the bars, or (*b*) dismounting
from the shoulder balance by means of an overswing dismount. The latter is done by partly flexing the hips in the
balance position, at the same time removing the hand grasp
on the bar and quickly flexing the elbows so that arms and
forearms grip the bar. As the body rotates forward the hips
are vigorously extended and the arms push away from the
bar. The landing is made with back towards the bars.

SHORT DESCRIPTION OF EXERCISE: *Toward outside standing facing centre of bars. Undergrasp and mount to balance
support. Pivot forward to lie across the bars and mount to
shoulder balance. Dismount by reverse order of movement
or by overswing. Plate* 9, facing page 48, shows across shoulder
balance.

Teaching points: A supporter may assist by standing between the bars and with the pupil lying across them, placing
one hand on the pupil's back, at the nape of the neck, and
the other either on his lower abdomen or behind the buttock-
fold when the pupil commences to flex his hips. He is thus
able to stabilise the shoulders on the bar at the same time
as he assists the pupil into a balance tuck position on the bar.
He should stay between the bars when the pupil, later,
attempts the extension to a shoulder balance proper, and
render necessary support. The method of support for the
overswing dismount is shown in *Plate* 11, facing page 48. It
will be noted that the supporter stands facing at right angles
to the path of movement and then supports by placing the
near hand under the pupil's shoulder, i.e. on the shoulder
crest, thus being able to impart 'lift', whilst the other hand
is placed at the base of the pupil's neck so that support and
guidance may be given without interfering with the angular
movement of the pupil's hips.

11. *Starting position: Toward Outside Standing facing
centre of bars.*

Combined grasp (left hand over and right hand under).
From this position by facing slightly to the left the pupil
swings his left leg under and up between the bars; the right
leg quickly joins the left and by extending the hips an up-

shoot is performed between the bars and the pupil finishes with his buttocks resting on top of the far bar, still retaining the hand grasp as before. The upshoot is aided by a vigorous pull-push arm action but the body-drape over the far bar is not held and the movement is continued, without pause, by swinging the right leg over in a wide arc on to the bar which the hands are grasping; at the same time the body twists to the left as the arms pull-push the trunk up above the bars. The pupil now finishes in an astride sitting position across the bars, the left hand being transferred on to the left bar as the sitting position is attained. The whole movement must be smoothly and continuously performed throughout.

SHORT DESCRIPTION OF EXERCISE: *Toward outside standing facing the centre of the bars – combined grasp; shoot-through to across back lying on opposite bar; pull-push with arms and body-turn with right leg circling over to astride sitting across the bars. Optional finish.*

Teaching points: First practise the shoot-through to back lying on the far bar. When this part has been mastered go on to attempt the pull-push with leg circling over to astride sitting. The hardest part of the exercise is the pull-push of the trunk above the bars, but if the leg is swung over vigorously enough this will assist the elevation of the trunk. A supporter may give some assistance by helping the pupil to get above the bars, i.e. on the transition from *pull* to *push* which is the most difficult part of the exercise. This is a most impressive movement when well done and is a very good introduction to an exercise sequence on the bars.

12. *Starting position: Toward End Standing facing end of bars.*

Grasp bars and spring to support position; raise both knees then, rounding the back, bend arms and tucking chin on to chest, perform a forward-roll on the bars. The elbows must be kept well out from the sides so that the actual roll is done on the upper arms. The legs are kept tucked well up throughout and, as the hips begin to fall forwards-downwards, the hand grasp must be quickly changed from rear to front. At this point the body is in tuck position with all the weight being borne by the backs of the upper arms resting on the bars. The arms now pull strongly as the roll continues and the weight is transferred from the upper arms on to the hands and back again on to the upper arms as continuous rolls are made. This is a quite difficult movement which demands good arm, shoulder, abdominal and hip-flexor strength. Care must be taken not to let the body unroll, otherwise the increased length of lever resulting from this will make the movement too difficult to accomplish. Later however, with increasing strength and skill, the pupil will be able to perform several continuous rolls in a piked position, i.e. with straight legs instead of in a tuck position.

SHORT DESCRIPTION OF EXERCISE: *Toward End Standing. Mount to support position on bars and continuous tuck, forward rolls along the bars.*

Teaching points: The forward-roll on the bars should follow mastery of the straddle-roll, already described. It is necessary initially to provide some support and this is best given by a supporter standing outside the bars and giving some 'lift' and rotation to the pupil as he attempts the movement. This support must be applied from *beneath* the bars by pushing up on the pupil's shoulders as he rolls on to his upper arms. The supporter must never place his arm across the bars as the weight of a heavy pupil dropping on the supporter's arm could cause some serious injury to it. As an extra precaution it is a good plan to have a thick mattress pad on the base of the bars in case of a fall.

13. *Starting position: Toward End Standing.*

Grasp bars and spring to support position at the same time swinging the legs forward-astride and placing a leg over each bar (astride sitting). Keeping the legs very straight and with toes well pointed, grasp the bars about one foot distance in front of the thighs – about opposite the knees. Now, by pulling with both arms, bend the trunk forward to place the upper arms on the bars, keeping the elbows pointing well out from the sides of the body, and with head pressed well back. Keep a firm grip of the bars and lift to a shoulder balance. The legs may be tucked up at first, if desired, or kept straight but the latter is much more difficult to do.

SHORT DESCRIPTION OF EXERCISE: *Sit astride the bars at*

end, facing in. Grasp in front and lift to upper-arm or shoulder balance on bars.

Teaching points: Practise first to rock up to a momentary balance, allowing the upper arms to contact the bars and returning to astride sitting. Later, rock up and tuck legs well up when the seat is directly over the shoulders, hold the balance and slowly extend the legs to attain an extended shoulder balance. The final stage is to rock up with legs perfectly straight in a pike position and, keeping the legs straight, slowly extend the hips to attain the shoulder balance. Support must be given in the early stages and the supporter/spotter must be on the alert in case the pupil slips down between the bars. Stress keeping the elbows pointed well out from the sides so that the upper arms take the body-weight. When the movement has been mastered, the pupil may return from the balance position to astride sitting, or, alternatively tuck up and perform a forward-roll along the bars finishing in either astride sitting across the bars or in side sitting on one bar – legs outside the bar.

14. *Starting position: Between Standing at centre of bars.*
Grasp bars and spring to support. Now, keeping the legs perfectly straight, raise the legs up in front to a half-lever position, i.e. with toes about level with the lower chest. Now, by rotating the head and trunk forwards-downwards, elevate the hips, maintaining the piked position, and place the upper arms on the bars. Next, with straight legs, extend the hips and hold a shoulder/upper-arm balance on the bars.

SHORT DESCRIPTION OF EXERCISE: *Between support at centre of bars; half-lever press up to upper-arm balance on bars.*

Teaching points: Initially, try the movement with the knees tucked well up towards the chest – it is much easier this way.

15. *Starting position: Support position at end of bars facing in.*
Swing between bars and on a backward swing bend the arms and swing up to a shoulder balance. You may do this by

maintaining a hollow-back throughout or with a slight bending of the hips which makes the movement easier.

SHORT DESCRIPTION OF EXERCISE: *Support position at end of bars facing in.*

Teaching points: Practise swinging with increasing momentum elevating the legs on the backward swing and bending the arms at the same time as the feet reach peak height behind. Check the movement as the shoulders near the bars, opening out the elbows at the same time, and bringing elbows in to the sides on the return swing. Finally attempt to hold the shoulder balance. A supporter should always be standing-by outside the bars to check rotatory movement if necessary but the pupil always has the remedy of folding at the waist and continuing the movement as a straddle-roll.

16. *Starting position: Toward End Standing.*

Grasp bars and mount to support position; swing up to a shoulder balance on the bars then, by pushing up with the arms, attempt to get to a short-arm balance, returning to shoulder balance. Practise this movement until proficient and then attempt to swing up straight away into a short-arm balance.

SHORT DESCRIPTION OF EXERCISE: *Support position at end of bars facing in; swing up to shoulder balance; push up to short-arm balance and return again to shoulder balance.*

Teaching points: These are as for the previous exercise but note that strong and good performers are able to press up from the short-arm balance to a full-arm (long-arm) balance.

17. *Starting position: Support at end of bars facing out.*

Swing between bars and perform a short-arm hollow-back overswing dismount from the bars, to land with back towards bars. See *Plate* 10, facing page 48, showing hollow-back, short-arm overswing dismount.

SHORT DESCRIPTION OF EXERCISE: *Support at end of bars facing out: swing, and hollow-back overswing dismount.*

Teaching points: This is more difficult than the piked overswing in which there is a substantial bend at the hips – the hips lead the movement. Practise first to swing up to a

PLATE 7. Showing forward astride dismount over both bars
PLATE 8. Front support thigh rest

PLATE 9. Across shoulder-balance
PLATE 10. Hollow-back short-arm overswing-dismount

PLATE 11. Showing method of support for short-arm over-swing dismount

PLATE 12. Elbow lever to short-arm balance

short-arm hollow-back balance then later, with more vigour
and the assistance of a supporter, attempt the complete movement. *Plate* 11, facing page 49, shows the method of support
for this.

18. *Starting position: Support at end of bars facing out.*
Swing between bars and at the end of the back-swing part
the legs and flex the hips to finish sitting astride the bars –
legs straight and toes well pointed. Now, still grasping the
bars in front, lean back to the full extent of the arms and
lower the seat until level with the top of the bars. From this
position heave strongly with the arms to pull the head and
trunk forwards-downwards, at the same time rocking up the
seat in a rotatory movement. Keep the arms fully bent and
stabilise the arm and shoulder joints – head pressed well
back – until the hips move forward in advance of the hands
on the bars. Then, as the piked hips move forwards-downwards, vigorously extend the hips and thrust away strongly
with the arms to perform a piked, bent arm overswing dismount from the end of the bars. The legs, from their astride
position on the bars, meet in the mid line as the hips rock up.
    SHORT DESCRIPTION OF EXERCISE: *Astride sitting across
bars facing out. Piked, short-arm overswing dismount from
end of bars.*
    Teaching points: The legs must be kept straight through-
out the movement and all the body-weight is taken on the
insides of the thighs until the hips rock up, when it is all
transferred on to the hands. Support for the overswing is
provided by a supporter standing at the end of the bars,
facing across, and as the performer reaches the inverted pike
position the supporter places outside hand on the base of
the performer's neck and grasps the pupil's upper arm with
his other hand. He can then give support and 'lift' and, by
maintaining hand contact throughout, can guide him to a
safe landing.

19. *Starting position: Support position at end of bars
facing out.*
Swing between bars and mount to a short-arm balance.
Hold the position momentarily and then thrust vigorously

down with both arms to push the head and chest upwards and initiate a backward rotation. As the legs swing down towards the bars, part them quickly, at the same time flexing the hips, and perform an astride cut-off dismount over the ends of the bars. By pushing away vigorously with the arms, a good aerial position may be obtained before a landing is made in a standing position with the back towards the end of the bars.

SHORT DESCRIPTION OF EXERCISE: *Short-arm balance at end of bars, facing out. Astride cut-off dismount.*

Teaching points: Master the swing up to the short-arm balance first. Then push up with the arms and part the legs to sit astride the bars – legs straight and insides of thighs almost touching the hands on the bars. Control the movement by tightening arms and shoulder muscles so that the thighs come to rest lightly on the bars. When the complete movement is being attempted for the first time a supporter must stand at the end of the bars facing the performer, and a little to one side. The supporter must then grasp one of the pupil's upper arms with both hands (inward grasp) and as the performer attempts the cut astride he steps backwards one pace, lifting and pulling the performer clear of the bars. Although this looks a difficult feat, it is not really as difficult as it appears.

20. *Starting position: Upper-Arm Hang at centre of bars.*
Note: The bars should be sufficiently high so that the pupil in the upper-arm hang position should have his feet well clear of the base of the bars. His elbows should be slightly bent with hands grasping the bars in front, palms of hands on top of the bars and thumbs around.

Free body-swing between the bars, and as the legs swing forwards-upwards, press down with the arms on the bars to elevate the hips and bring the straight legs overhead so that an inverted piked position is reached. Hold this position with the flexed hips above the bars and then, by vigorously extending the hips (beating out and down with the legs), and pressing down strongly with the arms, attempt to get to a support position on the bars. This type of movement is called an upstart. It needs plenty of practice and is a movement in which good timing is required. The extension of the hips and downward beat of the legs are checked as the arms press and pull. The sudden checking of the downward beat tends to push the trunk upwards and the upthrust is assisted by the press-pull of the arms so that the pupil finishes in support position. See *Fig.* 18 (1-5) showing upper-arm upstart to rest.

SHORT DESCRIPTION OF EXERCISE: *Upper-arm hang at centre of bars. Upper-arm swing and upstart to support position.*

FIG. 18. Upper-arm upstart to rest. Follow the sequence from left to right. *Note* simultaneous leg beat and arm press. Timing is important here. Reversing the sequence, (right to left) will give a swing drop back to pike upper arm rest.

Teaching points: As a lead up to the complete movement practise an upper-arm swing bringing the legs overhead, as described, to hold a piked position on the bars. Now beat down with the legs, at the same time parting them to wide astride, and press-pull with the arms to reach an astride sitting position across the bars. This is a much easier movement to do and when he has mastered it, the pupil should experience little trouble with the more difficult skill. A supporter may assist the performer in the initial learning stages by pushing up on the pupil's back as he beats up to support.

21. *Starting position: Support at centre of bars.*

Swing between bars and as the legs swing up in front, continue by bringing the straight legs overhead. At the same time allow the trunk to drop back on straight arms, so that the upper arms come to rest on the bars as the legs reach their overhead position. This is the inverted piked position described in the previous exercise and from here an upstart may be made to reach the original starting position, i.e. support position. Various continuative movements may be added, e.g. instead of finishing in support position the pupil may continue by swinging straight into a short-arm balance on the bars, or again, if he so desires, into a quick pike followed by a piked forward-roll along the bars terminating with a short-arm overswing dismount. *Fig.* 18 (a-c) shows swinging drop-back to upper-arm pike rest, followed by *Fig.* 18 (c-a) upper-arm upstart to rest/support.

SHORT DESCRIPTION OF EXERCISE: *Support at centre of bars. Swing and drop-back bringing legs overhead to pike position or pike rest. Upstart to support.*

Teaching points: Practise the swinging drop-back to pike rest until proficient. Initially this is a little alarming but the pupil soon gets used to it and if he bends his elbows slightly outwards as he nears the bars he will render the chances of slipping down between the bars less likely. Later, the upstart to astride sitting may be attempted before the upstart to support. It should be noted that upper-arm hangs and drop-backs are exceedingly painful to the arms and may cause some bruising. It is a good thing therefore, to wear a thick, long-sleeved pullover with perhaps some kind of foam sewn into the inside of the upper arm. Even without this kind of protection the pupil soon gets toughened to the work and will eventually feel little discomfort. The same applies to the insides of the thighs when they forcibly contact the bars. Many pupils give up such movements because of the initial physical discomfort.

(E) MORE ADVANCED SKILLS ON PARALLEL BARS

1. *Starting position: Upper-Arm Hang at centre of bars.*
Upper-arm swing with increasing momentum and on a

forward swing allow the legs to swing up overhead. At the same time as the body rolls on the upper arms, release the hand grasp and extend the semi-flexed arms sideways, throw the head well back and hollow out the back by vigorously extending the hips and shooting the legs straight up overhead. The performer has now reached what is virtually a shoulder balance on the bars; he quickly re-grasps the bars in front, and continues the hollow-back roll. If desired, the momentum from the first roll may be used to perform further rolls or, alternatively, the pupil may remain in the original upper-arm hang position by checking and controlling the downward swing with his arms, after re-grasping the bars.

Variations of this skills are backward-roll to astride sitting and backward-roll to short-arm balance or shoulder balance.

SHORT DESCRIPTION OF EXERCISE. *Upper-arm swing at centre of bars and backward-roll to finish in original starting position.*

Teaching points: First practise high upper-arm swings with increasing height. At peak height attempt to hollow out to shoulder balance then quickly bend at the hips and return to starting position again. Alternatively, continue through the balance point, quickly grasping the bars in front of the chest and descend to a support position or astride the bars. It is difficult to provide support for this particular movement but a spotter must be in attendance in case of accident and, as always, vital protection must be given to the head.

2. *Starting position: Upper-Arm Hang at centre of bars.*

As for the previous exercise, the pupil from an upper-arm swing performs a back-roll and, at the high point when the body is completely extended with feet directly overhead, the hands quickly grasp the bar in front of the chest. As the roll continues the weight passes from the upper arms on to the hands so that by pushing up with his arms as the extended body rotates backward, the pupil comes to rest in a support position on the bars.

SHORT DESCRIPTION OF EXERCISE: *Upper-arm swing and back-roll to support.*

3. *Starting position: Upper-Arm Hang at centre of bars.*

Swing between bars and when sufficient momentum has been developed as the legs rise above the level of the bars behind, quickly separate the legs to wide astride. As the arms heave vigorously to pull the head and trunk up above the bars, quickly snap the legs forward above the bars in a straddle movement by flexing the hips. As the arms heave and push the trunk up above the bars the legs sweep forward towards the hands which momentarily release their grasp of the bar for the legs to pass and then quickly re-grasp again. The legs meet in the mid-line and then swing down between the bars. In the early stages of learning it will be best to prac-tise the uprise first, i.e. as the legs reach peak height on the backward swing the arms heave the head and trunk above the bars so that a support position on the bars is reached. Next, part the legs on the uprise and finish in astride sitting across the bars. Follow this by practising the complete move-ment with hand release and re-grasp, by making use of a pre-liminary thigh bounce on the bars in the straddle position. Lastly, attempt the complete movement without the legs touching the bars at all. This is very difficult to accomplish. The thigh bounce allows just that extra bit of lift and assis-tance needed to complete the movement in the early stages of learning.

SHORT DESCRIPTION OF EXERCISE: *Upper-arm swing, back uprise and straddle-double forward circle of both legs over bars – to support.*

Teaching points: Upper-arm swings can be very painful and the pupil should not be kept practising too long at a time. Having taught the uprise, then get the pupil to part his legs at the end of the back swing – one leg over each bar – so that he reaches a straddle forward lying position on the bars. Follow this by allowing the pupil to heave with the arms, partly flexing the hips when the legs are astride. It is difficult to give any assistance with this exercise and simple progressive stages are the answer to complete mastery of the movement.

4. *Starting position: Support at centre of bars.*

With the thumbs on top of the bars, close to the index fingers, raise the straight legs forward by flexing the hips until the eyes are looking directly at the feet in front, i.e. feet at about upper chest height. Now, keeping the arms straight, allow the trunk to fall backwards, at the same time bringing the legs a little closer to the body, i.e. increasing the hip flexion, and pendulum-swing beneath the bars. After mastering this fairly simple movement attempt to get to upper-arm rest by beating out and down with the straight legs at the end of a back swing, simultaneously pressing down with the straight arms. As the shoulders rise above bar level the elbows are quickly flexed and moved outwards to place the upper arms on the bars, whilst the legs swing backwards-downwards between the bars. Later, this simple upstart movement can be practised so that instead of finishing the movement in upper-arm rest position, the pupil finishes in support position on the bars.

SHORT DESCRIPTION OF EXERCISE: *Support at centre of bars – thumbs on top of bar. Pike drop-back and pendulum-swing beneath bars followed by upstart to upper-arm rest.*

Teaching points: The most difficult part of this movement is the drop-back because if the elbows are bent, even very slightly, there is a risk of striking them on the bars as the drop-back is made. It is best, therefore, to practise the drop-back and pendulum-swing at the end of the bars, facing in. In this way there is no danger of striking the elbows on the bars. There is however, especially with old type bars, a danger of striking the hips on the uprights of the bars during the drop-back, depending, of course, on the size of the performer. It must also be borne in mind that the thumbs must be kept on top of the bar close to the index finger. If the bar is gripped by the thumb when the drop back is made, some damage or injury may be caused to the thumb joint.

5. *Starting position: Toward End Standing.*
Grasp the bars – hands on top and thumbs touching index finger (false grasp). Now lean away from the bars to the full extent of the arms, feet about one foot distance away from the base of the bars and hips flexed. From this position, swing one leg quickly forwards-upwards and, with a thrust from the supporting leg, swing that leg swiftly upwards to join its partner overhead. The body should now be in an acutely

piked position and swinging, like a pendulum, on straight arms. The extent of the swing may be increased by little pumping movements of the straight legs, from the hips. On one of the back swings press down strongly with both arms on the uprise, at the same time beating out and down with the straight legs to upstart to support position.

SHORT DESCRIPTION OF EXERCISE: *Toward end standing – false grasp. Backward lean with straight arms and from a pendulum-swing between bars; upstart to support. (Upstart to support at end of bars.)*

Teaching points: The essence of this skill is timing and this comes with long practice. A spotter may assist the movement by giving the pupil some lift on the uprise. This may be done either by grasping one of the pupil's upper arms with both hands on the uprise, or by thrusting upwards on the pupil's back as he rises to the support position.

6. *Starting position: Upper-Arm Hang at centre of bars.*

Upper-arm swing and on a forward swing allow the legs to swing well up in front by bending at the hips. As the feet approach the high point, sharply extend the hips thus shooting them out, down and back, at the same time heave-press with the arms to pull head and trunk above the bars and, as the legs swing backwards, stop in support position or between rest.

SHORT DESCRIPTION OF EXERCISE: *Upper-arm swing at centre of bars – forward uprise to support.*

7. *Starting position: Upper-Arm Hang at centre of bars.*

This exercise is similar to the previous one only that the uprise is performed at the end of the back swing of the legs, instead of on the forward one. The same principles apply and, as the feet reach peak height behind, the hips are quickly flexed and then as quickly checked after a short flexion. At the same time the arms heave and then press the head and trunk up above the bars so that a support position is reached.

SHORT DESCRIPTION OF EXERCISE: *Upper-arm swing at centre of bars – back uprise to support.*

(F) ADVANCED BALANCING AND OTHER SKILLS

Before attempting to hand balance on the parallel bars the beginner should master two things:

(a) He should be able to hold a good balance on the low parallel bars – about six inches high. These can be easily made by any handy man.

(b) He must have put in a great deal of practice at high swinging on the high bars. Attempting high swings to hand balance on the bars can be very dangerous indeed unless there has been adequate training under proper supervision beforehand. It is wise to proceed with caution and the beginner will find the following stages very useful.

(i) Mount to support at centre of bars and practise a free shoulder swing between the bars, keeping the legs straight and together and taking care not to let the legs swing up too far in front. There is an optimum height beyond which the swing has to be forcibly checked by tightening arm and shoulder muscles. This inhibits free body-swinging and the forward swing of the legs should be checked when the feet are a little above bar level; they should then be swung forcibly downwards-backwards to gain sufficient impetus to take the performer up to a hand balance position. Initially, however, the backward swing of the legs should be checked when a little above bar height behind. The following downwards-forwards swing is controlled by checking with arm and shoulder muscles and flexing a little at the elbow joint if necessary.

(ii) Next, try taking small swinging hops forwards and backwards alternately, i.e. as the legs reach peak height in front, hop forward on the hands and again, hop backwards when the legs reach the end of the backward swing. This is a useful exercise and the ability to do this may be the means of preventing an accident or fall following too vigorous a swing up, or a swing which is badly controlled.

(iii) Gradually increase the arc of the swings to above the horizontal behind, then checking the return swing.

Follow this by swinging up to a near hand balance with a slight bending of the elbows as the legs swing overhead. This slight bending of the elbows facilitates inversion of the body, the arms being straightened again as balance point is reached. However, before this point is reached, check the upward movement and swing back down to support or to body-swing between bars. The return-swing must be equally well controlled for if it is not, and the legs swing too high in front, a backward rotation of the trunk could follow with the performer falling back on to the bars.

(iv) A very useful exercise is to place the parallel bars with one end against a wall. The pupil stands on the bars facing the wall and about one yard away then, bending down, he grasps the bars at a distance of about eighteen inches from the wall and kicks up to a hand balance with both feet resting against the wall. A supporter standing on the floor on the outside of the bars assists the pupil to mount up by grasping the pupil's upper arm with the hand nearest to the wall and placing his other hand flat on the pupil's upper chest. The supporter is thus able to stabilise the pupil and at the same time push up on his chest as he attempts to kick up to hand balance.

When the pupil has mastered this simple skill he may then attempt, by hand pressure, to bring his feet away from the wall to attain a free-hand balance. This may be followed by the pupil taking one or two steps backward along the bars and then forward again. By these means the pupil gains in confidence and skill and is soon able to progress to more difficult movements.

It is always wise when practising the movements described, to have a mattress or other suitable padding material placed on the base of the bars in case of a fall. In any case, all these movements should be closely spotted.

(v) When the pupil is sufficiently confident to attempt the free swing up to a hand balance he should try it first from a support position at the end of the bars, facing

out and the bars should be low enough for two supporters, one on either side, to reach up and grasp the
waist band of the pupil's shorts or trousers with the
near hand whilst the other hand grasps the pupil's
upper arm and stabilises the position. Sometimes all
that is necessary is for the supporter/s to place the outside hand at the base of the pupil's neck and the inside
hand on the pupil's lower abdomen or chest as he
rotates upwards to a hand balance.

Having completely mastered these preliminary
skills the pupil may proceed to learn the following
more advanced skills.

1. *Starting position: Support position at centre of bars.*
Swing up to a hand balance and as the balance point is
reached, make a quarter-left turn, pivoting on the straight
left arm; at the same time swing the right arm over to grasp
the opposite bar. The hand balance is held on the single bar.
If it is not possible to hold the balance position then the arms
should be quickly bent, thus bringing the chest close to the
bar, head pressed back, and an overswing dismount performed. Should this dismount not be possible because the
body is falling towards the bars then the arms should be
quickly flexed, the back rounded and the knees raised, i.e.
tucked up body posture, the descent being checked and controlled by tightening arm and shoulder muscles; land on base,
between bars. Should, however, neither of these apply, and
the pupil finds himself falling over backwards away from the
bars, he must, very quickly, bring one hand away from the
bar and swing the arm forwards-upwards at the same time
pivoting away from the bar on the straight supporting arm.
The hips are flexed simultaneously with these movements
and a landing made in side standing position with the supporting hand still grasping the bar. See *Fig.* 19, showing
swing up to hand balance and dismount with half-left
turn.

SHORT DESCRIPTION OF EXERCISE: *Support at centre of bars
– swing up to hand balance with a quarter-left turn to hand
balance on single bar. Dismount by overswing or by descending between bars.*

Teaching points: First try the pivot movement in the hand balance position, on a low (ground) parallel bars. When this has been well mastered, attempt the same skill on a low ordinary parallel bars. Two supporters should, however, be present, standing outside the bars on the side towards which the turn is being made. The supporters can then stabilise the hand balance position as already described and the pupil should dismount by coming down between the bars to finish standing on the base. The supporters may help control the descent by grasping the pupil's upper arm with their outside hands and placing the near hand flat on the pupil's lower chest as he tucks up and descends. Supporters must always be present during the learning stages and it is stressed that spotting and supporting are highly skilled functions not to be lightly undertaken by untrained persons.

FIG. 19. Swing to hand stand and, without pause, dismount with half left turn. Left *Note* shoulders too far in front of hands; Centre *Note* centre of weight over supporting hand and arm.

2. *Starting position: Support position at end of bars, facing out.*

After one or two preliminary swings mount to a hand balance. Hold the position momentarily and then, bending the arms slowly, descend to a bent or short-arm balance. Hold again momentarily and then, first slightly flexing the hips before vigorously extending them again, perform an over-swing dismount to finish standing with back towards end of bars.

SHORT DESCRIPTION OF EXERCISE: *Hand balance at end of bars, facing out. Dismount through short-arm balance and overswing.*

Teaching points: Spot the hand balance and descent to short-arm balance, and guide and support the overswing dismount, placing near hand under shoulder crest and the other on base of neck. Lift and guide the movement.

3. *Starting position: Support at end of bars facing out.*

Swing up to a hand balance and allow the extended body to fall away on straight arms as if about to commence a straight-arm hollow-back overswing dismount. Immediately thrust down as hard as possible on the bars to send the head and trunk upwards, at the same time flexing the hips and parting the legs to wide astride position. Thus the piked body, as well as being projected forwards-upwards by the strong arm thrust, also rotates backwards, and the legs straddle the bars before coming to meet in the mid-line as the dismount is made. The body is fully extended prior to the landing.

SHORT DESCRIPTION OF EXERCISE: *Hand balance at end of bars facing out. Cut-astride dismount.*

Teaching points: Assuming that the pupil can hold the hand balance without support; the supporter will stand facing the pupil but a little to one side so that he may place both his hands around the upper arm of the pupil. As the pupil attempts the cut-astride, the supporter steps backwards one pace, lifting the pupil and at the same time pulling him forwards. Thus the chance that the pupil may strike his thighs on the bars during the descent is minimised.

4. *Starting position: Support at centre of bars.*

Swing up to a hand balance and, transferring the weight on to the left arm, make a quarter-left turn pivoting on the left arm. When making the turn and transferring the body-weight, release the grasp of the right hand cautiously and gradually so that the tips of the extended fingers contact the bar last before the right arm is swung over and the hand grasp is transferred to the left bar. The balance is held momentarily before a further quarter-left turn is made and the balance is now held on both bars again. Later, a complete left or right turn may be made by practising rhythmical and even timed quarter turns.

SHORT DESCRIPTION OF EXERCISE: *Hand balance at centre of bars – rhythmical quarter-left/right turns, i.e. from balance on both bars, quarter turn to hold balance on single bar, then again on to both bars, etc.*

Teaching points: Practise quarter turns on low ground parallel bars first – there is little risk attached to this. Later attempt one quarter turn on the high bar hold momentarily and descend between bars. A supporter must always be standing by and he may best assist by stabilising the balance as previously described.

5. *Starting position: Support at end of bars facing out.*

Keeping the arms perfectly straight, raise both knees well up towards the chest-tuck position with back rounded. Immediately slightly bend the arms and, elevating the seat, attempt to press up to a hand balance.

SHORT DESCRIPTION: *Support at end of bars facing out: tuck-press up to hand balance.*

Teaching points: Again, practise first on ground parallel bars, but when attempting the feat on ordinary bars first try to get the flexed hips up to a position immediately above the hands. Next, straighten out the hips and knees, at the same time pushing up with the arms. It is important to remember not to push up with the arms until the hips are directly over the shoulders and hands, otherwise extension of the arms will result in the hips rotating backwards and the feat then cannot be accomplished. Again, remember that too much arm flexion coinciding with the hip rock-up or elevation will make it very difficult indeed to accomplish the press up. A supporter must stand in and may assist the pupil to press up to the hand balance.

6. *Starting position: Support at end of bars facing out.*

Keeping the arms straight, bend the hips and raise the straight legs up in front, toes well pointed, to a half-lever position. In this position, the straight legs are raised up in front until the toes are about level with the upper chest. Now, pivot forward and quickly semi-flexing the arms, rock the seat up and over the hands, still keeping the legs straight; then continue the movement by pressing up with the arms at the same time as the hips are extended and a hand balance finally held.

SHORT DESCRIPTION OF EXERCISE: *Support at end of bars facing out: raise legs to half-lever and press up to a hand balance.*

Teaching points: This feat again, is best learnt on the low bars before attempting it on the parallel bars. The feat requires excellent arm, shoulder, abdominal and hip flexor strength. The quick bending of the arms facilitates the hip rock up and there should be no pause – the whole movement must be smooth and continuous. Again, a supporter may assist the pupil by imparting some lift to the pupil's shoulders as he presses up. This is best done by the supporter standing outside the bars and placing his near hand under the pupil's shoulder, i.e. on the crest of the shoulder, whilst the other hand grasps the pupil's upper arm. The supporter may thus assist the press up and at the same time stabilise the movement. A more difficult version of this feat is one where legs and arms are kept absolutely straight throughout the whole movement. This feat demands great strength and is sometimes known as an Elephant Lift.

7. *Starting position: Support at end of bars facing out.*

Swing up to hold a short-arm balance and then press up to a full straight-arm hand balance.

SHORT DESCRIPTION OF EXERCISE: *Short-arm balance at end of bars facing out. Press up to a hand balance.*

Teaching points: This is a most difficult feat and requires

great strength. Beginners lacking strength in the arms will sometimes allow the legs to drop as the press up is attempted. The movement then cannot be successfully completed. It is best to have assistance from a supporter when attempted initially.

8. *Support at end of bars facing in.*

Swing up to hold a full hand balance and hand walk along the bars by transferring body-weight from one hand to the other as the steps are made. As the weight is taken by one arm, the hand on the opposite side is moved a short distance – about six inches forward, and this is continued until the end of the bars is reached. The pupil may then dismount by

(a) lowering to a short-arm balance and then performing an overswing dismount, or

(b) by performing a cut-astride dismount from the hand balance position, or

(c) by bringing one hand off the bar and swinging the arm forwards-upwards, at the same time pivoting on the other arm and making a quarter-right/left turn as the case may be – according to which hand is removed from the bar – to land in side standing to the end of the bars.

SHORT DESCRIPTION OF EXERCISE: *Support at end of bars facing in. Swing up to hand balance and hand walk along bars with optional dismount at the end.*

Teaching points: Do not take too long steps at first, otherwise there is a tendency to get into a straddle position of the hands – resulting in the pupil experiencing difficulty in moving either forward or backwards. He then has to move the forward hand back again to get from a position of mechanical disadvantage. There is sometimes a tendency for the pupil to bend at the knees and the sudden pull of the legs forces the pupil involuntarily to take several quick hand steps forward. This can be dangerous as the pupil may hand run along the bars and then fall over backwards. This must be watched for. Control is absolutely necessary and the legs must be kept perfectly straight throughout. Other faults are that the pupil may force his head back too much. As well as being a strain, this leads to increased hollow back – again a fault to be avoided.

When the pupil is learning this, a supporter must walk alongside him as he proceeds down the bars. He should stabilise if necessary – should the pupil show signs of imbalance – by grasping the pupil's upper arm with his near hand whilst placing his other hand flat on the pupil's chest. As an additional precaution, have a pad or mattress covering the base of the bars. Hand walking should first be practised on ground parallel bars.

9. *Starting position: Toward End Standing.*
Reach forward with the left hand and grasp the right bar – hand on top thumb on the inside of the bar. To grasp the bar in this way the hand must be turned so that the fingers are towards the chest; the forearm flexed to a right angle and the elbow elevated and pointing away from the chest. Now, with a spring and a pull-push of the left arm, make a half-right turn to mount to support position on the bars, facing out. As the jump-turn is made, the free arm is swung vigorously behind to assist the body turn and the hand quickly grasps the bar as the support position is reached.

SHORT DESCRIPTION OF EXERCISE: *Toward end standing – left hand grasping right bar in overgrasp. Half-right jump-turn to support position on bars, facing out.*

10. *Starting position: Toward outside standing facing centre of bars.*
Stand close to the bar and, reaching under the near bar, grasp the far bar with hands in overgrasp and shoulder width apart. With single leg leading, swing both legs under, up and over the far bar to perform an upward circle, at the same time pulling the chest in to the bar. Then as the body circles over the bar, push up with both arms to attain a front-leaning thigh rest across the bars.

SHORT DESCRIPTION OF EXERCISE: *Toward outside standing facing centre of bars. Reach under and overgrasp far bar: with single leg leading, upward circle to front-leaning thigh rest across bars.*

Teaching points: As the circle up is made, the wrists must be quickly twisted in order to get the hands above the bar, i.e. the heels of the hand must be on top of the bar so that the arms can press up to the rest or support position. If this is not done then the movement can not be completed successfully and the pupil ends up lying draped over the bars. He can then only complete the movement by altering his hand grasp and then pushing up to rest. The pupil may dismount to stand between the bars, still retaining his hand grasp, by taking most of his weight on to his arms and then bouncing his thighs off the bar a few inches. From the thigh rebound bounce he can then quickly bring his knees in towards his chest and snap his feet over the bar to land on the base of the bars.

11. *Starting position: Toward Outside Standing facing centre of bars.*

As for the previous exercise, reach under to grasp the far bar and upward circle to front-leaning thigh rest across the bars. Having learnt to dismount by thigh bouncing and descending between the bars, the pupil may now attempt the movement to clear both bars with his feet and land standing on the far side of the bars, with his back towards them. This feat is not as difficult as it would appear and is merely a progression on the former exercise.

SHORT DESCRIPTION OF EXERCISE: *Toward outside standing facing centre of bars: reach under and overgrasp far bar; upward circle to rest and dismount by thigh-bounce through-vault over both bars.*

Teaching points: The danger in this activity is that the pupil may not release his hand grasp as his legs come through, or he may release the grasp of one hand only and bring his feet over the bar to one side. It is important that the pupil must push away strongly with his arms so that when the feet actually cross over the bar the hands have already been released; the arms swung forwards-upwards and the trunk already being extended ready for the landing. A supporter may assist by standing facing the pupil – as he attempts the movement the supporter grasps the pupil's upper arm with both hands (inward grasp) and then pulls the pupil forward to ensure bar clearance. Later the pupil may attempt the movement unaided but always with a spotter in attendance. The pull-push action of the arms and the snap up of the knees towards the chest are simultaneous and the success of the movement depends more on the arm action than any other.

12. *Starting position: Toward Inside Standing at centre of bars.*

Overgrasp the bar with both hands, hands shoulder-width apart – and with a spring, bounce the hips up between and above the bar, keeping the knees tucked up towards the chest. As the seat rises above bar level lean the body-weight well over the semi-flexed arms. Then vigorously extending the hips, shoot the legs up, back and down, at the same time parting them to a wide astride position and pushing away with the arms. This is a back astride-vault over the rear bar and a landing is made facing the bars on the outside and with hands in overgrasp on the near bar.

SHORT DESCRIPTION OF EXERCISE: *Toward inside standing at centre of bars: Overgrasp-hands shoulder-width apart, back astride-vault over rear bar.* See *Fig.* 20, showing toward inside standing – and back astride-vault.

Teaching points: Let the pupil first practise to vault to a crouch position on the rear bar. Next, vault to stand astride on the rear bar with hands still grasping the front bar. When

FIG. 20. Toward inside standing and back astride vault. *Note* vault to crouch or straddle stand on bar first as a leading-up stage.

these stages have been mastered let the pupil attempt the complete movement with a supporter standing between the bars. As the pupil vaults, the supporter may give assistance by placing one hand flat on the pupil's lower chest or abdomen, as he attempts bar clearance, in order to give some lift and to assist the bar clearance.

(G) ADVANCED CONTINUATIVE SKILLS— SEQUENCE MOVEMENTS

When pupils have mastered several single skills on the bars they may then proceed to link some of these together to form sequences with one exercise continuing smoothly and uninterruptedly into another. Thus the range of combinations of skills is vast and ensures necessary variety in the work. The pupil may devise his own sequences and practise them until perfect in performance; moreover, this type of work is a challenge to his ingenuity and a great deal of fun may be had from devising movements which may be quite original and enterprising.

Here are some examples of such sequences. They are not entirely original, neither are they comprehensive in scope. They serve merely to give some idea of what can be done by the average pupil.

1. *Starting position: Toward End Standing.*

Grasp the bars and spring to support position, at the same time swinging the left leg forward between the bars, on to the left bar close to the left hand. Release the grasp of the left hand and, pivoting on the left thigh – keeping the leg as straight as possible – make a quarter-right turn to place the left hand on the right bar. At the same time as the quarter-right body turn is made, swing the right leg up between the bars and place this leg on the left bar alongside the left leg. A front-leaning thigh rest is now reached. From this position release the grasp of the right hand and make a further quarter-right turn to assume an outside side sitting position on the left bar – left knee bent and right leg extended straight down. Place both hands behind and grasp the bars, then, taking the body-weight on to the arms, swing the legs forward upward and back down between the bars. Swing between the bars and on a backward swing, face-vault over the left bar, quickly bringing the right hand away from the right bar and transferring to grasp the left bar as the extended body passes over it. The landing is made in side standing with the right hand grasping the near bar.

2. *Starting position: Toward Outside Standing facing the centre of the bars.*

Grasp the near bar with overgrasp – arms fully extended and hands shoulder-width apart. Now vault to front-leaning thigh rest across the bars transferring first the left hand, then the right hand to the far bar as the spring is made. Forward circle of the left leg over the bar and then up between the bars to the right, at the same time releasing the grasp of the right hand and making a quarter-right body-turn, pivoting on the right thigh and with the leg perfectly straight. The left leg is swung over on to the right bar, the hips are flexed and an outside side sitting position taken up on the near bar. From this position, with left hand grasping the far bar and with the right arm held free behind the body, flank-vault over the far bar, swinging the right arm forward and grasping the far bar with the right hand as the extended body passes over it. Finish standing with back towards the bars.

3. *Starting position: Between Standing at centre of bars.*

Spring to support position and commence a body-swing: when the legs are forward, cross the left leg under the right leg and right circle of left leg backward along the right bar, releasing the grasp of the right hand for the leg to pass, transferring the body-weight on to the left arm and then quickly re-grasping with the right hand after the leg has passed along the bar. Continue swinging between the bars and as the legs are forward, rear-vault in front of left hand with a quarter-right turn to finish facing the left bar and with both hands grasping it with overgrasp.

4. *Starting position: Toward Outside Standing facing centre of bars.*

Reach forward and grasp the near bar with overgrasp –

hands shoulder-width apart. Vault to front-leaning thigh rest across the bars as described in exercise 2, page 69, at the same time circling the left leg to the right over the near bar. The left leg then hangs straight down and, from this position, the relative positions of the legs is changed by swinging the left leg well up to the left between the bars and then on to the bar, at the same time swinging the right leg to the left and down between the bars. The positions of the legs are thus reversed, this movement being called a back shears left. Continue by making a quarter-right body-turn and circling the right leg at the same time over the near bar to finish in an outside side sitting position on the bar – left knee bent, right leg straight down. Now place both hands on the bar behind and, swinging the legs well up in front and then down between the bars, perform a face-vault behind the left hand with a quarter-right turn to finish standing facing the bars with the hands in overgrasp.

5. *Starting position: Toward End Standing.*

Grasp bars and spring to support position at the same time circling the left leg inwards over the end of the left bar, i.e. right circle of left leg over end of left bar, and swinging the right leg forwards-upwards between the bars and placing the straight leg on the right bar. Extend the hips, at the same time making a half-left body-turn, transferring the grasp of the right hand to grasp the left bar and removing the grasp of the left hand as the body-turn continues. The left leg is swung backwards to make a half-left circle and the whole movement is finished in an outside side sitting position on the right bar, right knee bent. Place hands behind and grasp bars; swing legs well up in front and down between the bars. On the back-swing, perform a face-vault behind the right hand to finish in side standing, left hand grasping the near bar.

6. *Starting position: Toward Outside Standing facing centre of bars.*

Grasp near bar with overgrasp – hands shoulder-width apart – and spring to front-leaning thigh rest across the bars, transferring one hand at a time to the distal bar and at the same time half-right circle of left leg over the near bar. Most of the body-weight should now be resting on the arms and should be well over the hands. Swing the left leg well up to the left, between the bars and cross the right leg under it (back shears left). The left leg now rests on the bar with the right leg hanging straight down. Now swing the right leg high to the right between the bars and cross the left leg under it. The right leg now rests on the bar with the left leg down between the bars. Release the grasp of the right hand and make a quarter-right body-turn, swinging the left leg up to the right between the bars and then over on to the far bar (the left bar) to sit astride the bars with hand grasping the bars behind. Now swing both legs up in front and back down between the bars; on the ensuing forward swing rear-vault in front of left hand with a half-right turn, to finish in outside side standing with left side of body towards the bars.

7. *Starting position: Toward End Standing.*
Grasp bars and spring to a support position. At the same time swing the left leg inwards over the end of the left bar and then down between the bars, continuing into a body-swing and swinging up to a double-shoulder balance – both shoulders resting lightly on the bars and elbows pointing outwards. From the balance position tuck chin in to chest, bend hips and knees simultaneously, rounding the back and then roll forward on to the right bar, finishing in an outside side sitting position with the left knee bent. Grasp the bars behind and swing legs well up in front and down between the bars, swinging up into a short-arm balance on the bars. As the balance position is approached push away with the right hand and make a quarter-left turn, at the same time transferring the grasp of the right hand on to the left bar. The short-arm balance is now held momentarily on the single (left) bar, before the hips are slightly flexed and an overswing dismount performed from the single bar.

8. *Starting position: Toward End Standing.*
With a quick step forward between the bars spring on to upper arms and grasp the bars in front. As the arms contact the bar, the legs should be well up behind to initiate a body-

swing, i.e. upper-arm swing on the bars. Allow the legs to swing well up in front and perform a forward-uprise to support. Swing in the support position and allow the legs to swing above head height in front, at the same time dropping backwards on straight arms to upper-arm pike rest on bars (see *Fig.* 18). Immediately perform an upper-arm upstart, followed by a swing up to short-arm balance. Change to shoulder balance, fold to a pike position and roll to sit astride the bars, moving the hand grasp from rear to front as the roll is performed. Grasp the ends of the bars in front and with straight legs, toes well pointed, rock up to a short-arm balance at the end of the bars bringing the straight legs, from their astride position, together overhead. Hold the balance and then by pushing up and away strongly with both arms, perform an astride cut-off dismount over the ends of the bars. Land with back to the bars.

9. *Starting position: Toward End Standing.*

Spring on to upper arms and body-swing between bars (bars set high so that feet are well clear of the base) then perform a backward roll to return again to upper-arm swinging. Continue the roll and swing, by swinging both legs overhead to a piked position and perform an immediate upper-arm upstart to support. Swing between bars and rear-vault in front of left hand with a half-right turn, to finish standing facing the bars.

10. *Starting position: Toward End Standing.*

Spring on to upper arms and perform a back uprise to support/rest; at the same time as the uprise takes place swing the right leg over the right bar behind hands. Follow this immediately with a quarter-left body-turn to place the right hand on to the left bar to front-leaning thigh rest and perform a back shears left, i.e. swinging the left leg to the left and passing the right leg under it so that the left leg rests on the bars and the right leg hangs down between. Immediately swing the right leg to the right over the right bar, at the same time making a quarter-right body-turn to assume an outside side sitting position on the right bar, left knee bent. Perform, without pause, a flank-vault over the left (far) bar and land with back towards the bars.

11. *Starting position: Towards End Standing.*

Grasp bars and spring to support/rest, at the same time circling the left leg inwards over the end of the left bar and swinging the right leg forwards on to the right bar. Make a quarter-left turn, placing the right hand on to the left bar, and make a back shears left to place the left leg on the bar instead of the right leg. Continue the swing of the right leg to the left between the bars, at the same time making a further quarter-left turn. Place the right leg over the off bar to assume an astride sitting position across the bars – facing the end. Grasp the bars behind and swing the legs well up in front and back down between the bars, at the same time hopping backwards on the hands as the legs swing back; swing forward again. Right circle of the left leg backwards along the right bar, swinging the right leg backwards between the bars and leaning the body-weight well forward over the hands. Swing forward again and place the left leg forward on to the left bar. With a half-right body-turn place the left hand on to the right bar and half-circle of right leg to outside side sitting, left knee bent. From this position swing the free right hand over on to the off bar and perform an overswing dismount from this bar to land with back to bars.

12. *Starting position: Toward End Standing.*

Grasp ends of bars and leaning well back to full extent of arms, perform a short underswing upstart to shoulder balance on the bars. Bring chin in to chest, fold at waist bringing the feet down towards the head and roll forward on the right bar to outside side sitting. Place hands on bars in front and elbow lever to horizontal support. Continue through the elbow lever to short-arm balance on both bars. Lower legs to assume a support position and then raise both straight legs forward to half-lever support. Hold this position with toes about level with the face and make a quarter-left turn, still holding the lever position. As the turn is made release the grasp of the right hand from the right bar and pivoting on the left arm. Transfer the grasp of the right hand to the left bar and dismount by vigorously extending the hips, shooting the legs forwards-downwards and pushing away strongly with both arms. Land with back towards bars. See *Plate* 12, facing page 49, showing elbow lever to short-arm balance.

13. *Starting position: Toward Outside Standing at centre of bars.*

Reach forward and grasp bar with combined grasp, right hand in undergrasp. Now face-vault left over the near bar, transferring left hand on to far bar as the vault is made and finishing in swinging support position on the bars. Allow the legs to swing well up in front, drop-back on to upper arms as legs travel overhead, and perform an upper-arm upstart to double-shoulder balance on bars. Roll forward to sit astride the bars and, grasping the end of the bars, swing the legs up behind and in between the bars. Continue the swing into a full hand balance, lower to short-arm balance; pike slightly at the hips and perform an overswing dismount to land with back towards bars.

14. *Starting position: Toward End Standing.*

Grasp ends of bars and with a spring mount to support, quickly parting the legs as the spring is made and performing an inward circle of both legs over the ends of the bars (astride cut-in). Continue the movement by swinging the legs, together, down between the bars and up to a short-arm balance; fold at the waist and roll forward to astride sitting. Place the hands on the bars in front and lift to a short-arm balance; fold again and roll to an outside side sitting position on the right bar. Grasp the ends of the bars, moving closer in order to do this if necessary, and with a good heave and body-swing perform an overswing dismount to land with back to bars.

THREE

HORIZONTAL BAR WORK

Horizontal bar exercises demand a great deal of physical strength, enough to be able to handle one's body-weight with ease. This is because all such exercises start either from a full-arm hang poition, followed by a heave swing, or from a front support position on the bar. Both of these fundamental positions are quite difficult feats in themselves but only preliminary to the exercises which follow.

High bar work is therefore unsuitable for young children and they should first receive some practise and training on the low bar where they may use their legs to gain initial impetus for the heave swings and upward circles, etc. To begin with, the bar should be at about shoulder height, or perhaps a little lower, but as the pupils get better and stronger the height may be increased to about head-height when more effort is required to accomplish some skills.

This type of work may be made quite as interesting as high bar work for many of the high bar skills may be equally well performed on the low bar. However, there are some low bar skills which cannot with safety be performed on the high bar, e g. overswing dismount which can easily be performed on the low bar cannot be done on the high bar because of the greatly increased height – about eight feet or more at full height.

It is frustrating and discouraging to beginners of any age when they are initially introduced to the high bar for they find that when hanging at full arm stretch from the bar they can do little more than ineffectually kick their legs, lacking the strength to pull up to an upward circle or perform a heave swing.

Most children love to swing on bars or ropes and there is therefore no real reason why young children should not be taught simple bar work in junior schools, thus establishing a good foundation for more advanced work at the secondary school stage. Most junior schools have a type of horizontal bar in the playing field or playground but they are usually much too thick for any serious work to be attempted on them. Besides, they are usually erected over hard surfaces – a calculated risk in my opinion – unless the bars are very low and a good layer of padding is placed beneath them.

Thick bars are extremely dangerous for performing swinging movements on. A suitable bar for general use is one of about three inches in circumference, enabling children to grasp the bar so that the thumb may touch the forefinger easily. Any bar which is of such thickness that this cannot be done, is much too thick for safe work. Galvanised bars are suitable for outdoor work but they should be wiped dry befor being used. Although not ideal for advanced work a great range of skills may be performed on them.

GENERAL ADVICE ON BAR WORK

Before commencing to deal with all the skills which may be performed on the low and high bars some hints and advice, of a general nature, are essential.

1. The thumbs must be around the bar always, i.e. the bar must be grasped so that fingers and thumb completely encircle the bar. The thumbs – with one or two exceptions – must never be on top of the bar alongside the fingers. It can be very dangerous if this rule is not adhered to.

2. When making complete *forward* circles around the bar the hands must be in *undergrasp*. In *backward* circles the hands must be in *overgrasp*. This is a golden rule and there is only one exception to it – this will be referred to later in the text.

3. Swinging, hanging or circling movements must never be performed over concrete bases or similar hard surfaces. For outdoor work it is recommended that the concrete blocks in which the uprights are set should be at least one foot beneath the surface, and the whole landing area, for a distance of eight feet each side of the uprights, should be a sandpit with a minimum depth of sand of eighteen inches. There is then little danger of a child receiving a serious injury should he or she fall from the bar. Equally important is the fact that the children have much more confidence to practise circles on the bar when they know that there is a soft landing.

Outdoor bars are easily made and cheap to provide. Several such bars around the perimeter of a field give endless fun and healthy outdoor exercise to children of all ages. In addition, the provision of several bars enables the children, after they have been trained in the rudiments of mutual aid methods, to be given a large measure of freedom to practise movements already taught. The following exercises will be found suitable for children in junior and secondary schools.

LOW BAR WORK

Bar at chest or head height:

1. *Starting position: Stand facing the bar – Overgrasp with hands about shoulder-width apart.*

With a spring, mount to front rest support position on the bar with arms straight, body extended, toes pointed and body inclined forward with the weight forward over the hands. Swing the legs slightly forward and then vigorously backwards. At the end of the swing push strongly away with the arms to dismount standing facing the bar, i.e. in the original starting position. Repeat this exercise using firstly undergrasp and then a combined grasp, i.e. one hand in undergrasp and the other in overgrasp.

SHORT DESCRIPTION OF EXERCISE: *Toward standing-overgrasp: spring to front rest and dismount with legs swinging backwards.*

2. *Starting position: Stand close to bar – undergrasp with hands just about shoulder-width apart.*

With the arms semi-flexed, lean away from the bar, then swing one leg forwards-upwards over the bar – quickly followed by the other leg. At the same time heave the chest strongly close in to the bar, throw back the head to assist backward rotation began by the vigorous leg action and, as the legs pass over the bar, sharply flex the hips so that the abdomen contacts the bar and the downward swinging legs then assist the elevation of the trunk; the extension of the arms and back and hips bring the pupil to a front support position on the bar.

SHORT DESCRIPTION OF EXERCISE: *Toward standing-over-grasp; upward circle to front rest. See Fig.* 21.

Teaching points: The above method of performing this exercise enables the pupil to get thrust from the supporting leg and rotation from the upward swinging free leg. These factors make the movement easier to accomplish than if the pupil was hanging from a high bar.

Variations of this exercise are

(*a*) Upward circle with overgrasp – this will be found much more difficult than with undergrasp.

(*b*) With combined grasp, i.e. one hand under and the other hand overgrasp.

(*c*) Using a double take-off instead of a single-footed take-off.

Assistance may be given to the pupil, when first practising the movement, by a supporter placing one hand on the shoulder crest and the other on the back of the hips and giv-

FIG. 21. Upward circle to front rest.

ing some lift and rotation to enable the pupil to circle up on to the bar. Some pupils will find this movement difficult because they have weak hip-flexors and abdominals. These pupils will probably use the impetus method at first, or will require manual assistance until they develop sufficient strength to perform the movement unaided.

3. *Starting position: Toward Standing-Overgrasp with hands shoulder-width apart.*

Spring to front rest on bar then, bending the arms, fold at the hips, bend the knees, round the back and, tucking chin on to chest, perform a forward circle downwards to hang with knees tucked up to chest. Lower or extend hips and legs slowly and dismount.

SHORT DESCRIPTION OF EXERCISE: *Toward standing-over-grasp: spring to front rest and forward circle dismount.* See *Fig. 22.*

Teaching points: This is not a difficult exercise to perform as gravity does the work; the pupil however must control the speed of descent and must perform the movement with caution in the initial stages. A supporter should be standing by and should check the speed of descent if necessary. He does this by taking some of the pupil's weight at hip level by placing one hand on the back of the pupil's hips as he rotates forwards-downwards; the other hand is placed on top of the pupil's hand on the bar. This form of support may soon be dispensed with for all but the very poor performers.

FIG. 22. Forward circle dismount from rest.

4. *Starting position: Toward Standing-Overgrasp with hands shoulder-width apart.*

Spring to front rest/support and leaning trunk well over the hands, turn a quarter left between the hands to place the right thigh and buttock on the bar – the other leg hangs straight down. This is side sitting position. When balance has been achieved the hand grasp may be released and the arms stretched straight down or extended sideways. Follow this by re-grasping the bar and then make a further quarter-left turn to back support. Do not sit on the bar but extend the hips and then by bending the arms slightly get the bar to contact the back just above the buttocks. Now arch the back and, allowing the head to drop back, rotate backwards until the inverted body is supported only by the arms. This position is known as inverted hang or reverse hang. Next, flex slowly at the waist and allow the legs to drop until the body is fully piked – legs may be kept straight or tucked up whilst this movement takes place. Rotate backwards to the full limit of the shoulder joints until the pointed toes touch the floor and dismount by releasing hand grasp.

SHORT DESCRIPTION OF EXERCISE: *Toward standing-over-grasp: mount to front support; change to side sitting, then to back support and dismount by backward circle, to finish standing facing bar. Fig. 23a shows side-sitting position. Fig. 23b shows back hang balance. Fig. 24 shows back hang position.*

FIG. 23. (*a*) Showing side sitting position; (*b*) Showing a back hang balance.

Teaching points: The teacher or supporter should stand on the same side of the bar as the pupil is when he is in the front support position. He may then assist the pupil to make his turns by grasping the pupil's thigh, just above the knee, with his left hand, whilst grasping the pupil's waist band with his right hand. The teacher must be on the look out for any signs of imbalance when the pupil is attempting the turns on his own and quickly steady him by grasping one of his legs. When the pupil performs the backward circle dismount the supporter should stand behind the pupil and place his near hand under the bar and on top of the pupil's hand on the bar. He then places his other hand on the pupil's upper abdomen in order to take some weight and thus control the speed of descent. The hands must be kept in overgrasp throughout.

PLATE 13. Showing commencement of 'Windmill'

PLATE 14. Showing sitting position on bar preparatory to seat-circle backwards

PLATE 15. Showing starting position for mill circle forwards. Note undergrasp

PLATE 16. Leap to bar and drop-back undershoot – dismount

PLATE 17. Showing trampette bounce overswings – in stream

5. *Starting position: Toward Standing – hands in Over-grasp and shoulder-width apart.*

Mount to front support and lean body-weight forward over the hands, keeping the arms straight. Now take all the weight on to the right arm and make a half-left turn to back support, releasing the grasp of the left hand and swinging the left arm quickly around to re-grasp the bar in overgrasp as the body-turn is completed. Change grasp of right hand to overgrasp and backward circle dismount to stand.

SHORT DESCRIPTION OF EXERCISE: *Mount to front support: half-left turn to back support: change to overgrasp and backward circle dismount.*

FIG. 24. Showing back hang position on completion of back circle dismount.

Teaching points: Keep weight well over hands as the body-turn is made. Keep arms straight throughout. The backward circle dismount must be spotted during learning stages. Variation of this exercise: Make continuous half-turns along the bar and descend with either forward or backward dismount according to whether the movement is finished in front or back support. *Fig.* 24 shows the back hang position before dismounting.

6. *Starting position: Toward Standing-Overgrasp with hands shoulder-width apart: Mount to Front Support.*

Taking the weight of the body fully on to the straight arms, commence a lateral pendulum-swing from the shoulders, allowing the legs to swing well up from side to side. Finally swing the legs well up to the right and over the bar, releasing the right hand grasp for the legs to pass and at the same time transferring body-weight on to the left arm by leaning well over to the left side. As bar clearance is made, push away from the bar with the left arm, swinging the right arm sideways-upwards, and land with back towards the bar. This is known as a flank-vault because the side of the body passes over the bar as the vault is made. Ideally, the body, whilst supported by the perpendicular left arm should be parallel with the bar but, with beginners, a position approximating to this is acceptable. *Fig.* 25 shows flank-vault from front rest.

SHORT DESCRIPTION OF EXERCISE: *Toward standing-overgrasp: spring to front support: lateral body-swing and flank-vault, right, over bar.*

Teaching points: After practising the pendulum-swing, endeavour to swing both legs up to the right and come to rest

FIG. 25. Flank vault. Dismount from front rest.

in a side support position on the bar. As soon as the feet come to rest on the bar, release the grasp of the right hand, straighten the hip angle by elevating the hips and hold the position for a moment. Dismount by swinging the right arm and leg forwards-upwards and land with back towards the bar. A supporter may assist the pupil to hold the side support position on the bar.

7. *Starting position: Toward Standing-Overgrasp with hands shoulder-width apart.*

With a heave and a spring flank-vault over the bar. As a lead up to this, practise first to vault to side support on the bar – a supporter may hold the pupil in his position. It is then but a short step to learning the complete vault.

SHORT DESCRIPTION OF EXERCISE: *Toward standing-overgrasp: flank-vault over the bar.*

8. *Starting position: Toward Standing-Overgrasp.*

Mount to front support/rest, from a lateral body-swing, swing the legs up to the right as for a flank-vault and, as the legs clear the bar flex quickly at hips and knees to sit on the bar, at the same time re-grasping with the right hand. Now, keeping the knees raised, push up with the arms to raise the seat off the bar – all the body-weight will now be taken by the arms. At the same time project the seat backwards so that the backs of the flexed knees contact the bar. Without pause, stretch up as tall as possible, throw the head back and then drop backwards on straight arms to perform a three-quarter backward circle. At the end of this release the hand grasp and straighten out to land with back towards the bar.

SHORT DESCRIPTION OF EXERCISE: *Toward standing-overgrasp. Mount to front support: half-left circle of both legs to sitting followed by a three-quarter seat circle dismount.*

Teaching points: This is not a difficult exercise but it is important to remember that throughout the seat circle the arms must pull the flexed knees in close to the bar – or perhaps it would be more correct to say that the back must be kept extended in order to push the backs of the knees into the bar. If this is not done, contact with the bar will be lost and it will then not be possible to complete the movement successfully. Later a complete full circle back to sitting may be done. When attempting to get to the initial sitting position on the bar, a supporter may assist to stabilise the pupil in position by standing behind him and as the pupil gets to sit on the bar he, the supporter, by grasping the pupil's hips, with a hand on either side, can hold the pupil in position on the bar. At the end of the three-quarter circle the supporter should ensure that the pupil arrives to a safe landing by placing one hand on the pupil's chest and the other on his back, as the pupil is about to release his grasp of the bar and straighten out.

9. *Starting position: Toward Standing.*

Overgrasp the bar with hands at shoulder-width apart and then with feet directly under the bar, lean back to the full extent of the arms. From this position swing one leg swiftly upwards and then from a vigorous take-off of the supporting leg, swing that leg quickly up to join its fellow. As the piked body swings down, heave strongly with both arms, at the same time shooting the legs outwards and downwards by quickly extending the hips and arching the back. This extension of the body coincides with a strong arm thrust which serves to project the extended body outwards. As complete extension of body and arms is reached, the hand grasp is released and a landing is made with the back towards the bar. This movement is known as a heave undershoot.

SHORT DESCRIPTION OF EXERCISE: *Towards standing-overgrasp: backwards lean: with single leg leading heave undershoot.*

Teaching points: Stress the vigorous upward-swing of the legs and the pull-push action of the arms. Emphasise that landings should be made on the balls of the feet with 'give' at hips, knees and ankles.

10. *Starting position: Toward Standing-Overgrasp with hands shoulder-width apart.*

Perform an upward circle to front rest. Lean forwards over the bar, hollowing out the back and extending the legs behind. From this position, keeping the arms straight, swing the legs forwards-upwards under the bar to a pike position and, as the legs reach the end of the forward swing, drop backwards on straight arms, at the same time bringing the insteps close in to the bar. As the downward swinging flexed hips reach the end of their swing, vigorously extend the hips and shoot the legs up, out and down as described in the previous exercise. The whole body describes an arc in the air and a landing is made in a standing position with back towards the bar.

SHORT DESCRIPTION OF EXERCISE: *Upward circle to front rest: drop-back on straight arms and undershoot dismount.* See *Fig.* 26 showing front rest position and dismount.

Teaching points: First practise the drop-back and continue into a swing landing at the end of the back swing. Later practise to perform the upward circle, drop-back and undershoot without any pause throughout.

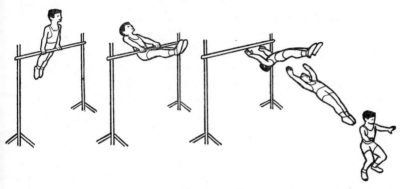

FIG. 26. Drop back undershoot dismount from rest.

11. *Starting position: Toward Standing-Combined Grasp, i.e. left hand in Overgrasp and right hand in Undergrasp.*

Spring to front support position on the bar and, with a quarter-right body turn, swing the left leg over the bar to astride sitting. The hands are now in inward grasp and should be kept close together and close to the body. Now extend the body, i.e. extend the hips and legs, then cross the ankles and grip the bar between the thighs. From this position initiate lateral body rotation by vigorously throwing head and trunk down to the right. At the same time, swing the legs upwards on the opposite side. The extended body will now rotate around the bar as a long lever, the pivotal points being the hands and the insides of the thighs where they contact the bar. This skill is sometimes referred to as the Windmill and beginners should not experience great difficulty in accomplishing it.

SHORT DESCRIPTION OF EXERCISE: *Astride sitting-inward grasp: ankles crossed – windmill or lateral circle. See Plate 13,* facing page 80.

Teaching points: No support is necessary for this simple skill but a supporter may assist by grasping the pupil's feet and spinning him around the bar, i.e. he gives some rotatory assistance.

12. *Starting position: Toward Close Standing-Overgrasp with arms full bent.*

With a spring, bring knees well up towards the bar, at the same time stretching the arms fully; continue the movement by bringing both feet between the hands and under the bar. Now extend the hip and knee joints a little and place the back of the flexed knees against the bar, then crook the knees over the bar by fully flexing the knees. Next, allow all the body weight to hang by the knees and cautiously release the hand grasp, extending the trunk until the body is hanging vertically, suspended only by the crooked knees. This position is called Hock Hanging or Knee Hanging. From this position a dismount may now be made by

(a) Looking back for the floor and then placing the hands flat on it; follow this by pushing up with the arms to take the weight off the knees, straighten the knees and then descend through a hand stand position.

(b) Dismount by re-grasping the bar, taking the weight fully on to the arms and perform the original movement in reverse, i.e. tuck knees well up, pass the feet forward under the bar and unroll to a hang position.

(c) Re-grasp the bar and dismount through a reverse hang, i.e. allow the legs and trunk to drop slowly backwards to the limit of movement in the shoulder joint – then release the grasp of the bar and drop off to standing. The latter movement is known commonly as skinning the cat.

SHORT DESCRIPTION OF EXERCISE: *Toward standing-overgrasp: upward circle to pass feet under bar, crook knees over bar, release hand-grasp and hock hang. Dismount via handstand, etc.*

Teaching points: Later, perform a handstand on the floor in front of the bar, kick up to a handstand, crook knees over bar and, removing hands from floor, take up a hock hanging position.

13. *Starting position: Mount to Hock Hanging on the bar by any of the means described, e.g. Handstand to Hock Hanging.*

Now initiate a body-swing by swinging the arms vigorously forwards, at the same time arching the back and then swinging the arms back again and slightly rounding the back; these movements will serve to gain a considerable swing. At the end of a forward-swing throw the arms forwards-upwards vigorously, strongly arch the back, throw the head well back and then extend the knee joints so that the legs come away from the bar; quickly flex the hips, swinging the legs forward. A landing should be made in a standing position with the back towards the bar.

SHORT DESCRIPTION OF EXERCISE: *Mount to hock hanging on the bar and dismount from a forward hock-swing.*

Teaching points: A partner may assist the beginner by helping him to gain sufficient swing; he may do this by pushing up on the pupil's chest on the forward-swing. When the dismount is being attempted the supporter can assist again, by pushing up on the pupil's chest as his legs leave the bar. This is all that is necessary in most cases and it is quite safe for a pupil to attempt this skill entirely on his own where a sandpit or thick landing pad is available.

Some children may be a little nervous at first, but demonstrate how easy the feat is by getting a pupil to hock hang from the bar then, facing him, place your hands under his arm-pits and lift him forwards-upwards until his body is almost horizontal. Whilst still supporting his body-weight instruct the pupil to straighten his knees and he will then drop into a standing position on the floor. Another simple demonstration with a pupil in the hock hanging position is to lift the pupil backwards until his back is almost horizontal then, releasing the pupil and thus allowing him to swing down, place a hand on his chest and run with him as he swings forward. At the end of the forward-swing with the supporter's hand still imparting some lift the pupil straightens his knees and lands in a standing position. Later, lift the pupil, as described, then release him and allow him to complete the movement on his own.

14. *Starting position: Toward Standing-Overgrasp with hands shoulder-width apart.*

With a spring, mount to front support and make a quarter-right turn to side sitting on the bar; make a further quarter-right turn to sitting. From this position push up with both arms to lift the seat clear of the bar, keeping the knees raised well up in front. Bring the back of the crooked knees in to the bar, keep the back straight and then throw back into a back seat circle. At the bottom of the swing pull in strongly with both arms, round the back, pushing the seat up and over the bar and at the same time quickly twist the wrists in order to bring the hands on top of the bar. The movement is completed in the original starting position and the movement may then, without pause, be performed several times in succession. See *Fig.* 27.

SHORT DESCRIPTION OF EXERCISE: *Sitting on bar with hands in overgrasp – seat circle backwards*. See *Plate* 14, facing page 80, showing sitting position on bar preparatory to seat circle backwards.

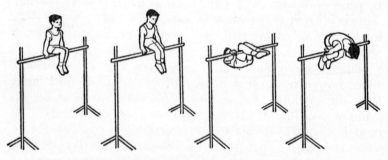

FIG. 27. Seat circle backwards. *Note* seat being pulled over bar on uprise.

Teaching points: Speed and timing are very important in this skill. The pupil must in all such movements remember to make himself as tall as possible above the bar and as small and compact as possible under the bar and on the uprise. The seat circle dismount should be practised first, and when this has been accomplished successfully the supporter may assist the pupil to achieve the full circle by standing at right angles to him on the uprise and with a hand on his near shoulder, pushing him up into a sitting position on the bar. Care must be taken however, not to push the pupil over the bar, and the supporter should check backward rotation, if necessary, by grasping the pupil's near ankle with his free hand as the pupil reaches a sitting position. Again, the supporter may assist by standing sideways on to the bar, near to the pupil as he sits on the bar. Then, passing his near arm under the bar, he grasps the waist-band of the pupil's shorts – if a safety belt is provided so much the better – and is thus able to assist the pupil's rotation around the bar. By pulling the pupil around with one hand and pushing up on the pupil's near shoulder on the uprise, the supporter can ensure that the pupil completes the movement successfully.

15. *Starting position: Sitting on the bar.*
Part the legs and grasp the bar centrally with hands fairly close together. Push up with the arms, keeping the crooked knees close in to the bar, and perform a seat circle backwards as in the previous exercise. See *Fig.* 28.

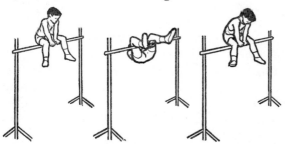

FIG. 28. Astride seat circle backwards.

SHORT DESCRIPTION OF EXERCISE: *Astride seat circle backwards.*

Teaching points: All the points mentioned for the previous exercise also apply to this one. Most pupils prefer this method of seat circling because they find it easier to get the seat up and over the bar on the uprise.

16. *Starting position: Sitting on bar, knees together and hands in Undergrasp.*
As in the previous exercises, push up with the arms to take all the weight and bring the backs of the crooked knees tight in to the bar. From here, circle forward and around the bar until the original starting position is reached.

SHORT DESCRIPTION OF EXERCISE: *Sitting, knees together: undergrasp: seat circle forward.*

Teaching points: The knees must be kept against the bar throughout. There is a tendency during the forwards-downwards movement for the legs to come away from the bar and control is then lost. As with the previous exercises, the pupil must make himself tall above the bar and small beneath it. On the uprise care must be taken not to pull in too sharply with the arms, otherwise if the uprise is not sufficiently far advanced, the net result will be that the body is pulled in to the bar and the circle-up is checked. Any jerky movements should be avoided; as the head and trunk rise up above the bar the pupil must press down with his arms to supplement the uplift. It is necessary during the learning stages to have a supporter standing behind ready to give the pupil some 'lift' on the uprise. He may do this by pushing up on the pupil's buttocks as the circle is completed.

17. *Starting position: Mount to Front Support Undergrasp: place right leg over bar between hands.*

From this position, bend the right knee and keep the back of the thigh pressed tightly against the bar with the other leg stretched straight down behind. Now push up with the arms to make yourself as tall as possible, keeping the back of the front thigh against the bar and the rear leg held away from the bar. Vigorously throw head and trunk forwards-downwards and circle around the bar back to the original starting position. The forward impetus and the swing up of the rear leg behind should be sufficient to ensure completion of the circle and a return to the starting position.

SHORT DESCRIPTION OF EXERCISE: *Mount to front/forward astride sitting undergrasp: mill circle forward.* See *Plate* 15, facing p. 80, showing starting position for mill circle forward. Note undergrasp.

Teaching point: Instruct the pupil to press down with his arms on the uprise and to extend his hips. If the hips flex during the uprise the pupil will just fold on to the bar and he will not then be able to get on top of it.

18. *Starting position: Mount to Forward Astride as in previous exercise (but Overgrasp instead of Undergrasp).*

This exercise is basically the same as the previous one

except that a backward, instead of a forward circle, is performed. Again, as in the previous exercise, the knee of the front leg is flexed and the thigh pressed hard against the bar. The hips must be extended to get maximum height above the bar and, coinciding with the throw-back or cast-away to commence backward rotation, the rear leg which until now has been held a few inches away from the bar, is swung vigorously forwards-upwards to assist rotation. Again, the principle of making the body compact underneath the bar on the uprise is important to the success of the movement.

SHORT DESCRIPTION OF EXERCISE: *Front astride sitting-overgrasp: mill circle backwards.*

Teaching points: The whole movement is started by a quick extension of the arms to push weight above the bar; following this, the trunk and head are thrown back to commence backward rotation whilst the rear leg is swung vigorously forwards-upwards. Impress on the pupil the need for speed and vigour. The final effort to get back up on top of the bar is the most difficult part: on the uprise the back must be rounded, the free leg shot vigorously over the bar and the wrists quickly twisted to get the heels of the hand on top of the bar and thus in position to enable the pupil to push up to the original starting position. A supporter may assist the pupil to complete the movement successfully by pushing up on his chest or shoulders on the uprise. When one circle has been mastered, several may be continuously performed.

19. *Starting position: Toward Standing-Overgrasp with hands shoulder-width apart.*

Mount to front rest/support on the bar by any means, e.g. upward circle to front rest. Now, keeping the arms straight, swing the straight legs forwards-upwards to a pike position and then drop backwards on straight arms keeping the insteps close to the bar as the full flexed hips swing forwards under it. As the hips swing back again – insteps still close to the bar – beat downwards with the straight legs and at the same time press downwards strongly with the straight arms. The downward swing of the legs is suddenly checked before extension of the hips is completed and this sudden check has an uplifting effect on the trunk which, aided by the downward pressure of the straight arms, rises above the bar. Following the leg-check and uprise, the legs are then swung backwards to give a rotatory effect to the extended body which then pivots forwards on the hands, enabling the performer to gain a rest position on the bar. This feat is known as a short upstart or, as the American's term it, a kip up. The success of the movement is 'timing' and much practise is necessary before success is assured.

SHORT DESCRIPTION OF EXERCISE: *Front rest: pike drop-back and upstart to rest.*

Teaching points: As the chest rises above the bar on the uprise – not sooner – the arms may be flexed a little to pull the chest over the bar as the legs swing back. If this arm flexion takes place too soon, i.e. before the upper chest is well above bar level, the pupil pulls himself in towards the bar and the movement is 'killed'. A supporter may assist by timing the pupil's leg beat and pushing up on his back on the uprise.

This particular skill may be used in combination with other movements, e.g. front rest, drop-back upstart followed by a hip circle backwards and under swing: dismount at the end of the back swing with a half-right turn.

20. *Starting position: Full-Arm Hang-Overgrasp: Hands close together.*

Crook the right knee over the bar close to the right hand, keeping the shoulders parallel with the bar – do not allow them to swing away at an angle to it. Now, by swinging the free leg vigorously forwards and backwards, initiate a body-swing. Finally, from a very vigorous back swing of the free leg with a simultaneous pull-push of the arms, endeavour to get on top of the bar to a forward astride position. This is known as a single-leg acting upstart.

SHORT DESCRIPTION OF EXERCISE: *Single-leg acting upstart or single-leg circle-up with knee outside hands to forward astride sitting.*

21. *Starting position: Full-Arm Hang-Overgrasp.*

Raise both knees and crook the right knee over the bar between the hands. From here, perform a single-leg acting upstart to forward astride sitting or astride rest, as described in the previous exercise.

SHORT DESCRIPTION OF EXERCISE: *Full-arm hang with overgrasp – hands shoulder-width apart: single-leg acting upstart to forward astride sitting, knee between hands.*

Teaching points: This exercise is basically the same as the previous one but some find it easier to perform because of the more balanced starting position on the bar. The pupil may be assisted in the initial learning stages by a supporter pushing up on his buttocks as he attempts the uprise. Again, by timing the movement expertly, he may grasp the free leg just above the knee and thus assist by giving the pupil a 'leg up'. Additional movements may be added from the forward astride rest position, e.g. the pupil may continue immediately into a back mill circle, followed by a drop back and withdrawal of the leg continuing into an underswing dismount.

22. *Starting position: Mount to Support position on the bar. Overgrasp.*

From this position circle the left leg forward over the bar to assume a forward astride support position. Next, half-left circle of the right leg to sit on the bar, the right hand being removed for the leg to pass, and then re-grasping the bar. Push up with the arms to take the seat off the bar and, at the same time, raise the straight legs forward to a half-lever position, i.e. the straight legs are raised forward until the toes are level with the chest. Hold this position momentarily – for it is a very difficult position to hold – and then dismount by quickly extending the hips and shooting the legs forwards-downwards, at the same time pushing away powerfully with the arms. Land with the back to the bar.

SHORT DESCRIPTION OF EXERCISE: *From support on the bar with overgrasp: half-right circle of left leg: half-left circle of right leg to sitting: raise legs forward to half-lever and dismount with legs shooting forwards-downwards and push off from arms.*

23. *Starting position: Full-Arm Hang-Overgrasp and Hands shoulder-width apart.*

Crook right knee over bar between hands and circle up to forward astride rest; immediate half-right circle of right leg to assume a support position and perform a straight leg, pike drop-back with undershoot dismount.

SHORT DESCRIPTION OF EXERCISE: *Full-arm hang: right leg crooked over bar between hands: single-leg acting upstart to rest: half-right circle of right leg and drop-back undershoot dismount.*

Teaching points: Transfer weight on to left arm and remove grasp of right hand as leg circle is made. The whole movement should be performed without pause.

24. *Starting position: Toward Standing-Overgrasp with hands wide apart.*

Spring to rest position and lean chest forward over the bar so that some of the weight is taken by the thighs, i.e. front-leaning thigh rest. Now swing both legs backwards to take the hips away from the bar – about six inches – and then swing them vigorously forwards-upwards so that the lower abdomen, just above the pubis, contacts the bar. As the legs swing forwards-upwards the trunk rotates backwards so that the whole body rotates backwards as a long lever with but a slight bend at the hips. At the end of the circle the head and trunk arch back, at the same time as the arms straighten to assume the front rest position again. See *Fig. 29.*

SHORT DESCRIPTION OF EXERCISE: *Mount to forward rest-overgrasp: cast-away, i.e. swing legs backwards about six inches taking the hips away from the bar and hip circle backwards on return swing.*

Teaching points: The pupil should practise the cast-away first and he must be told to bend his arms slightly on the return swing so that the hips contact the bar at just the right place, i.e. just above the pubis. It is important to remember that the trunk should be actually rotating backwards as the hips contact the bar otherwise the pupil merely folds around the bar and the movement is killed. Many pupils are afraid to allow the trunk to rotate backwards as the legs swing up in front and then attempt to perform the movement slowly; this results in the pupil falling away from the bar. Speed is essential in this movement and the arms must pull the body into the bar throughout. Some assistance may be given the pupil when he is on a low bar, by a supporter pushing his hips into the bar as the pupil rotates around the bar. With practice and increasing confidence the pupil soon realises that success in this feat depends upon vigour and speed.

There are various variations and combinations of this movement, e.g. front rest – cast-away and hip-circle backwards to return to front rest; immediately drop back underswing dismount or after completing the hip circle and finishing in front rest, perform a half-left/right turn to back support and backward circle down to back hang or to hock hang – dismount through hand standing or hock swing off.

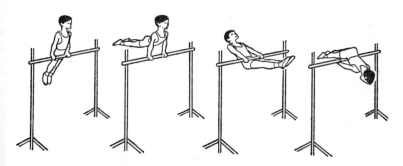

FIG. 29. Front rest: hip circle backwards. *Note* the preliminary cast away to obtain impetus.

25. *Starting position: Toward Standing-Overgrasp with hands shoulder-width apart.*

Spring to overgrasp hang and curl up to touch the bar with clear circle backwards, returning to the original starting position. This is essentially the same as the previous exercise except that the body does not touch the bar at all during the circle. This is a very much more difficult exercise to perform and a great deal of practice is needed before it can be mastered.

SHORT DESCRIPTION OF EXERCISE: *Front rest-overgrasp: cast-away and short clear circle backwards to return to starting position.*

Teaching points: The whole of the body-weight is borne by the hands which form the pivotal points. The wrists must be kept fixed and extended – should they flex as the body rotates then it will not be possible to complete the movement. There must be a definite wrist twist to get the heels of the hands on top of the bar; at the same time the head is thrown back and the back straightened to finish in Rest position. The feat should be practised on a low bar so that supporters may be enabled to give some assistance or to stand by. A supporter may assist by pushing up on the pupil's chest during the last quarter circle – on the uprise.

Variation: Short clear circle with shoot up to momentary handstand and then return to front rest. This is an advanced exercise and may be a preliminary to a grand circle around the bar. It is performed by the pupil on the last quarter circle, as the head and trunk are on the uprise, shooting his legs straight up above the bar, at the same time pull-pushing with his arms and then arching the back – the wrists are, at the same time, quickly twisted in order to get the hands on top of the bar so that the arms may be completely extended.

SHORT DESCRIPTION: *Front rest-overgrasp: cast-away and short clear circle backwards to handstand.*

Teaching points: With the bar at low chest height, two supporters may assist the pupil by standing in front of him, side-on, when the pupil is in a rest position on the bar. As the pupil attempts the shoot-up to handstand the supporters may grasp the pupil's upper arms with their near hand whilst the outside hands are placed on the pupil's back near the nape of the neck. They can thus stabilise the pupil on the bar, at the same time giving some 'lift' and assistance to enable him to gain the handstand position on the bar.

26. *Starting position: Mount to Front Rest with Overgrasp.*

Forward circle around bar to return to original starting position. The essentials of this difficult feat are speed and timing. The body moves around the bar, head leading and the movement is begun by pushing up with the arms to gain height followed by head and trunk being thrown vigorously downwards. The hips are kept slightly flexed throughout and on the uprise the wrists are quickly twisted to bring hands, wrists and elbows well above the bar. The trunk is

PLATE 18. Showing inverted hang position

PLATE 19. Crow's Nest

PLATE 20. Crow's Nest. Single hand and opposite foot

PLATE 21. Showing support/rest position on rings. Note arms locked against ropes for stability

PLATE 22. Pull-up to support and forward circle dismount to hang

PLATE 23. Backward hollow-back circle down to inverted hang from rest

PLATE 24. Forward astride cut-off at end of back-swing. Note supporter

then straightened and the hips extended as the arms push up to front rest.

SHORT DESCRIPTION OF EXERCISE: *Front rest-overgrasp: short clear forward circle.*

Teaching points: Speed and vigour are essential to this movement. The hips are semi-flexed throughout and any extension of the hips during the first three-quarter circle will prevent the movement being completed. Some assistance may be given to the pupil by a supporter pushing up on his seat on the uprise to front rest. It will be noted that overgrasp is used for this movement – not undergrasp as is usual for forward movements.

27. *Starting position: Sitting on the bar – legs wide astride: hands grasping the bar centrally and close together.*

Now push up quickly with the arms and at the same time extend the legs and push the seat up and away from the bar, bringing the backs of the heels on to the bar – the legs must be kept wide astride. Without pause, the movement is continued into a backward circle with the arms and legs quite straight. The body swings under the bar and continues into the uprise at the end of which the head is swung vigorously backwards, the hands release their grasp of the bar and the arms swing vigorously forwards-upwards as the whole body is extended. A landing is made in a standing position with the back towards the bar.

SHORT DESCRIPTION OF EXERCISE: *Sitting – legs apart – between overgrasp: backward three-quarter circle with heel-swing dismount.*

Teaching points: Teach the push-up and drop-back with three-quarter circle first. Tell the pupil to swing his head back to look for the floor at the end of the forward swing. Later, when the complete heel-swing dismount is being attempted, have two supporters standing behind the bar grasping the waistband of the pupil's shorts with their outside hands. As the pupil casts away and commences the backward circle, the supporters follow the movement throughout and maintain support until the pupil lands safely. The legs should be kept perfectly straight throughout and the swing should be fast and smooth. Hand release at the end of the forward swing must be simultaneous and at the high point of the swing. All segments of the body should then be vigorously extended so that the body has a good extended aerial position. If the legs are bent during the swing the pupil tends to be in a tucked up position when the bar is released and then lands in an ungainly position. The higher the bar, the easier it is to get a good body position in the air before landing. A suitable starting height for beginners is at about five feet.

28. *Starting position: Toward Standing – hands shoulder-width apart – Undergrasp.*

Perform an upward circle to rest and from this position quickly elevate the seat, by flexing sharply at the hips; get it as high as possible above the bar. At the same time, part the legs to wide astride and hook the insteps of the feet under the bar. Immediately commence a forward circle by tipping forward, keeping the arms and legs perfectly straight, and perform a three-quarter forward circle. At the end of this, allow the legs to drop and finish standing facing the bar. Later, the pupil may attempt the full forward circle but this is a very difficult feat and needs a great deal of practice and assistance.

SHORT DESCRIPTION OF EXERCISE: *Front rest-undergrasp: instep circle forwards astride.*

Teaching points: Seat elevation and the commencement of the forward circle must be continuous – no pause at all. Speed and momentum are vital to success and on the uprise the arms must press down very strongly in order to bring the piked hips up above the bar. Supporters may assist by pushing up on the pupil's flexed hips on the uprise.

29. *Starting position as for previous exercise.*

From this position elevate the seat quickly, bringing the knees up towards the chest and at the same time hooking the insteps under the bar. Immediately tip forward into a forward circle and at the end of a three-quarter circle lower the legs and, releasing the bar, drop off to land facing the bar. Later, the complete circle to front rest may be attempted.

SHORT DESCRIPTION OF EXERCISE: *Front rest-undergrasp: tuck, instep circle forwards with feet together.*

Teaching points: As in the previous exercise, speed, timing and vigour are the important factors. When the pupil makes his first attempts it is well to have a supporter standing in facing, and to one side of, the pupil. This is in order to give the pupil confidence to attempt the feat, for tipping forward with the toes hooked under the bar is a rather strange movement and usually gives the pupil a feeling of insecurity. Again, after the pupil has had several tries at the three-quarter circle, he should be given some assistance and 'lift' on the uprise when he attempts the complete circle. As in the previous exercise, a supporter may push up on the pupil's seat in order to assist him to get on top of the bar.

30. *Starting position: Front-Leaning Thigh Rest-Undergrasp.*

Bring the knees well up to the chest and place the soles of the feet on the bar. Perform a three-quarter forward circle, bringing the feet away from the bar at the end of the swing and finish in standing position facing the bar. Later, attempt the full circle with the assistance of one or two supporters.

SHORT DESCRIPTION OF EXERCISE: *Front-leaning thigh rest-undergrasp: place feet on bar between hands and sole circle forwards.*

Teaching points: This is not an easy exercise and many boys will be unable to get to the starting position, i.e. under-grasp crouch position on the bar, because they are not anatomically suited, i.e. arms too short to hold the position comfortably, or the leg levers too long. Commence by assisting the pupil to get to the starting position on the bar, if necessary, and then support him by holding the waist band of his shorts, as already described. Allow him then to attempt the three-quarter circle. Later, as the pupil gains confidence, he may attempt the full circle with a supporter giving support and 'lift' on the uprise. Instruct the pupil at the start of the circle, to push up with his legs, i.e. extend them, and then to bend them at the bottom of the circle and on the uprise in order to shorten the body lever, thus assisting forward rotation. The momentum gained from a vigorous swing, plus quick wrist twist and downward pressure of the arms, i.e. pull-press action, should be sufficient to bring him on top of the bar again. Supporters should be watchful to see that the pupil does not topple forward again when he gains the top of the bar and should instruct the pupil to shoot his feet forward off the bar and sit on it when the forward circle is completed.

31. *Starting position: Front-Leaning Thigh Rest-Overgrasp.*

Bring the feet on to the bar, as in the previous exercise, and immediately circle backwards. The same teaching points apply as in the previous exercise, and the essentials are speed, momentum and timing. Judicious support at the right moment is most important and helps the pupils to get the feel of the movement.

N.B. The last two exercises may also be performed with the legs in a wide astride position, and again, with the soles of the feet on the bar.

The foregoing should provide sufficient interesting and challenging skills to satisfy the needs of both master and pupil and, when completely mastered, will enable them to approach work on the high bar with a degree of confidence in their ability to cope and conquer.

FOUR

ELEMENTARY TO ADVANCED EXERCISES ON THE HIGH BAR

Whereas in low bar work the pupil was enabled to obtain power and impetus from contact with the floor, he now has to depend entirely on the muscular power of his arms, shoulders and trunk for gaining body-swing or for getting on top of the bar as, for example, in front rest. His feet, being clear of the floor when he is hanging from the bar at full-arm stretch, are unable to supply supplementary power, as in the case of low bar work. One may say, therefore, that the pre-requisite for high horizontal bar work is the ability of the pupil, when hanging from the bar, to pull up and chin the bar with ease and also to be able to curl up from full-arm hang to touch the bar with his toes or, better still, perform an upward circle to front rest. When he is able to execute these exercises easily he has the necessary strength to perform most exercises on the high bar for, as has already been mentioned, all such exercises commence with a heave-swing; from a full-arm hang position or from an upward circle to front rest.

For high bar work with juniors, the bar need not be at the full adult height of eight feet; it should be adjusted so that the tallest pupil in the group is able to swing on the bar at full arm's length with his pointed toes four or five inches clear of the mattress.

THE EXERCISES

1. *Starting position: Toward Standing.*
Spring to grasp the bar with overgrasp; hang to the full extent of the arms with body nicely extended and toes well pointed, eyes looking straight ahead. Dismount from the bar and repeat the exercise using the various grasps in turn, i.e. undergrasp, combined grasp (one hand in undergrasp and the other in overgrasp). *Fig.* 30, shows full-arm hang.

FIG. 30. Side hang. Full arm hang overgrasp.

2. *Starting position: Toward Standing.*
Spring to bent-arm hang, i.e. with the arms bent to a right
angle and hold the position for a moment or two before dismounting. Repeat this exercise using the other grasps
described.

SHORT DESCRIPTION OF EXERCISE: *Bent-arm hang.*

3. *Starting position: As for previous exercise.*
Spring to overgrasp hang on the bar near to the right hand
upright. Now release the grasp of the right hand and make
a half-left body-turn, swinging the right arm vigorously across
the body to re-grasp the bar at the end of the body-turn with
overgrasp. The left hand is now in undergrasp and the resulting position is combined grasp hang. Release hand grasp
and dismount.

SHORT DESCRIPTION OF EXERCISE: *Full-arm overgrasp hang
to right of bar: half-left body-turn to re-grasp (overgrasp) bar
with right hand.*

4. *Starting position: Toward Standing.*
Spring to undergrasp hang near the right hand upright
and, releasing the grasp of the right hand, make a half-right
body-turn, swinging the right arm around to the right, to re-
grasp the bar with overgrasp – both hands are now in overgrasp. Now release the grasp of the left hand and make a
further half-right turn to re-grasp the bar with the left hand
in undergrasp. Both hands are now in undergrasp. Release
hand grasp and dismount.

5. *Starting position: Toward Standing.*

Spring to overgrasp hang – hands shoulder-width apart and practise arm bending with alternate high knee raising.

6. *Starting position: Toward Standing.*

Spring to overgrasp hang and curl up to touch the bar with the toes. Hook the toes over the bar and cautiously release the hand grasp, being now suspended by the toes only. Do not extend the body at this stage but re-grasp the bar and lower legs to the original hand position. Dismount and repeat the exercise with the legs astride.

7. *Starting position: Toward Standing.*

Spring to overgrasp hang and curl up to touch the bar with the toes. Pass the feet under the bar between the hands and circle back to the full limit of the shoulder joints. Circle up again and extend the legs overhead, the inverted body being now completely extended and supported only by the hands. This position is reverse or inverted hang. Now curl up again and pass the feet forward under the bar to return to the original overgrasp hang position. Note: this exercise is sometimes known as 'skinning the cat'. See *Fig.* 24.

Repeat the previous exercise as far as the reverse (bent) hang, with the body hanging down to the full limit of the shoulder joints. Now taking a very firm grip with the right hand, cautiously release the grasp of the left hand. The body, now suspended only from the right arm, will slowly twist completely around to a single-arm hang position. Re-grasp with the left hand to finish in overgrasp hang. This feat is more a test of strength than skill but many boys will be successful at the first attempt.

8. *Starting position: Standing beneath the bar.*

Spring to overgrasp hang and perform a heave-swing. This is done by heaving with the arms to pull the chest up towards the bar, at the same time drawing the flexed knees up as high as possible. This movement is almost the same as the upward circle but as the feet near the bar the hips and knees are vigorously extended upwards and outwards at the same time as the arms pull-push to project the body outwards from the bar. Sufficient momentum is thus gained to enable the extended body to swing several times backwards and forwards on the bar. It will be apparent that the higher the leg-shoot and the stronger the pull-push action of the arms, the greater will be the momentum gained. A landing may be made at the end of the forward or the backward swing but caution must be used when attempting either of these dismounts for the first time. If, on the forward swing, the hand grasp is released when the body is rising, the pupil will land flat on his back. It is necessary therefore, when dismounting from a forward swing, to allow the legs to swing up in front by flexing the hips, and then arching the back and swinging the legs quickly downwards by a vigorous extension of the hips. The hand grasp is released as the legs are swung down, and the arms are then swung forwards-downwards from their overhead position. Similarly, on the backward-swing, the dismount is made by pressing down with the straight arms in order to bring the body to a near vertical position; the hips are slightly flexed and the legs swung forward at the same time as the arms push away from the bar and the hand grasp is released. This enables a landing to be made in a vertical position. Again, if the hand release was made when the whole extended body was rising in a wide circle the pupil would fly outwards from the bar and land flat on his face.

This is likely to happen with beginners and some time should be spent on showing pupils how to land following a heave-swing.

9. *Starting position: Standing underneath the bar.*
Spring to undergrasp hang and perform a heave-under-swing as described. On the second backward swing bring the body vertical by flexing the hips and pressing down with the straight arms. Whilst the body is still rising, quickly release the grasp of both hands simultaneously and re-grasp with overgrasp. Continue swinging and dismount at the end of the next back-swing with a quarter-left/right body turn, pushing away vigorously with the appropriate arm to effect the turn according as to whether it is to right or left. At the same time as the arm thrusts against the bar, the head is swung quickly around to assist the turning movement.

SHORT DESCRIPTION OF EXERCISE: *Heave-swing with under-grasp; re-grasp with overgrasp at end of back swing.*

10. *Starting position: Combined Grasp Hang.*
Perform a heave-swing and at the end of the back-swing release the grasp of the hand in undergrasp and change it to overgrasp. Dismount at the end of the back-swing.
SHORT DESCRIPTION OF EXERCISE: *Heave-swing with combined grasp.*

11. *Starting position: Toward Standing at right end of bar.*
Mount to overgrasp hang and perform a heave-underswing. At the end of the forward-swing release the grasp of the right hand and quickly make a half-left body-turn by swinging head, right arm and leg over to the left. Re-grasp the bar with the right hand in overgrasp. The left hand will now be in undergrasp. Continue into a forward-swing and dismount at the end of the ensuing back-swing.
SHORT DESCRIPTION OF EXERCISE: *Heave-swing with half-turns.*

12. *Starting position: Toward Standing at right side of bar.*
This is performed exactly as in the previous exercise but with the performer making a series of half-turns down the whole length of the bar. Each body-turn takes place at the end of a forward-swing, i.e. from the initial swing, a half-left turn is made at the end of the first forward-swing; a half-right turn on the next forward-swing and so on. A dismount is made at the end of the back-swing when the end of the bar is reached.
SHORT DESCRIPTION OF EXERCISE: *Continuous swinging half-turns.*

13. *Starting position: Toward Standing; Mount to Over-grasp hang.*
Perform a heave-swing and at the end of the first forward-swing quickly flex the hips, keeping the legs straight with toes well pointed, and bring the toes up to almost touch the bar. Immediately beat down with straight legs and at the same time press down vigorously with both arms. The combined

action of legs and arms should be sufficient to send head and trunk up above bar level and, as the shoulders rise above the bar, the pressure of the arms should be sufficient to pull the chest over the bar. A quick, slight flexing of the arms, to pull the chest inwards over the bar, is permissible at the learning stage but later the arms should be kept straight throughout. This movement is known as upstart and the pupil should finish in front rest/support position on the bar. It is unlikely however, that this will be achieved during the initial practices and a great deal of practice will probably be needed. This is an advance on the drop-back short upstart from front rest described in low bar work.

SHORT DESCRIPTION OF EXERCISE: *Heave-swing and upstart to front rest.*

Teaching points: The legs must be kept straight throughout, especially when beating down. If the legs are bent or the back rounded, much of the lift resultant upon the downward beat is lost and the movement will then probably fail. The arms too, must be kept straight until the chest rises above bar level – about ten to twelve – when the arms may be slightly flexed to pull the head and trunk over the bar. The essentials of this movement are controlled swing and good timing; the back must be kept straight throughout. A supporter may assist the pupil on the uprise by pushing up on his back as he attempts to gain the rest position. To do this, as the bar is a high one, he may need to have a platform to one side of the bar on which to stand to give the pupil support.

14. *Starting position: Toward Standing-Overgrasp Hang.*
Perform a heave-swing and at the end of the first forward-swing, swing the straight legs up to bring the pointed toes towards the bar; at the same time part the legs to wide astride and then, slightly bending the knees, bring the feet under the bar and place the backs of the heels against the bar, outside of the hands. Straighten the legs with the heels in the position described and continue to swing. Finally, withdraw the legs and lower them so that a hang position is reached. Then dismount.

SHORT DESCRIPTION OF EXERCISE: *Heave-swing to astride heel swing.*

Teaching points: The hips must be flexed and the feet brought in towards the bar when the hips are at peak height and just about to commence the return swing. If the hips are allowed to drop too far down it will not then be possible to bring the feet to the bar. This fact will become evident when the feat is initially attempted. Two supporters may assist the pupil by standing one on either side and grasping the waist band of his shorts – they may then guide the movement and at the same time safeguard the pupil. See *Fig.* 31.

FIG. 31. Heave swing and heel swing astride dismount.

15. Perform a heave-swing as in the previous exercise and finish off by dismounting from an astride heel-swing. This exercise has been described in low bar work but the following points need emphasising.

SHORT DESCRIPTION OF EXERCISE: *Heave-swing followed by an astride heel-swing dismount.*

Teaching points: The pupil should not merely drop off the bar at the end of the heel-swing: there must be a positive

and vigorous extension of the hips and back after the hand
release. In addition, vigorous extension of the head and a
forwards-upwards swing of the arms contribute to good body
extension and a good aerial position. It is important also, to
remember that it is the backs of the heels, not the backs of
the legs which should contact the bar. Also there must be
sufficient momentum to ensure a good body-swing so that a
good landing may be made. Supporters may give some assistance by supporting the pupil's chest at the end of the forward-swing, thus encouraging him to release his hand grasp.
This, many pupils are afraid to do, at first, and a little en-
couragement is sometimes needed. A sharp word of command
coinciding with the lift on the pupil's chest sometimes helps
considerably when he is perhaps prone to baulk at releasing
his hand grasp. Support may also be given by using a waist
belt with hand grips at either side, or again the waist band
of the pupil's shorts may be used instead; supporters using
either of these can take a firm grip when the pupil is in the
hang position and they may then follow the whole movement
throughout.

16. *Starting position: Toward Standing: Mount to Overgrasp Hang.*
Perform a heave-underswing and at the end of the second
forward-swing flex the hips quickly to bring both feet in to
the bar; bend the knees slightly and pass the feet under the
bar between the hands. By this time the flexed hips will have
reached the limit of the back-swing and on the return (forward-swing) bring the backs of the crooked knees in to the
bar and, on the uprise, increase hip flexion. Endeavour to
push the seat up and over the bar; at the same time pull in
strongly with the arms, twist the wrists quickly to get the
hands on top of the bar and then push up with the arms to
finish finally in sitting on top of the bar.
SHORT DESCRIPTION OF EXERCISE: *Overgrasp hang: underswing and, feet between hands, seat circle backwards to
sitting.*
Teaching points: This feat is not as easy as it sounds and
the following points should be noted: Allow the pupil to
practise the underswing and pike to bar first. Continue the

swing with the feet close to the bar and then dismount on a forward-swing by an undershoot dismount. Later allow him to practise a tentative seat circle, crooking the knees on the bar and dismounting at the end of the uprise by releasing the hand grasp and extending the hips, i.e. seat circle dismount as described in low bar work. The pupil will have previously mastered the seat circle from a sitting position on the low bar and all that he really has to master now, is the technique of performing the movement from a heave-swing instead of from a sitting position on the bar. A supporter may assist by pushing up on the pupil's chest on the uprise but when the pupil arrives in the sitting position the supporter should be ready to stabilise the pupil on the bar by grasping one of his ankles. This is because sometimes a pupil will commence a second circle inadvertently because of poor control and this must be watched for. Later, with increasing skill and confidence, several seat circles may be performed in succession.

17. *Starting position: Toward Standing: Mount to Overgrasp Hang.*

This exercise is performed in almost the same way as the previous one but instead of having the feet together and passed between the hands, the legs are parted as the pike to bar takes place and the seat circle is performed with the legs crooked over the bar outside the hands.

SHORT DESCRIPTION OF EXERCISE: *Overgrasp hang; heave-swing and astride seat circle backwards to sitting legs astride.*

Teaching points: Let the pupil practise the heave-swing and astride pike to bar first. Impress the necessity of keeping the backs of the knees pressed against the bar. The seat leads the movement and the hips must be kept fully flexed – any extension of the hips will mean that the pupil comes away from the bar and will possibly lock on to his arms. Teachers must watch for this and must assist in the early stages by helping the pupil to get to a sitting position on top of the bar. If the pupil has mastered the movement from sitting on the low bar, he will not experience great difficulty in achieving the seat circle following a heave-swing. Speed and vigour are essential ingredients of this feat.

18. *Starting position: Toward Standing-Overgrasp Hang.*
Perform a heave-swing and at the end of the first forward-swing quickly pike to bar, bend the knees slightly, passing the feet between the hands and under the bar. Quickly crook the knees over the bar and flex them strongly as the hips swing backwards. Continue the backward-swing and press pull with the arms on the uprise, rounding the back to bring head and chest up and over the bar. Finish in a sitting position on the bar. The sudden flexion of the knees plus the rotational speed and pull-push of the arms should be sufficient to enable the pupil to finish on top of the bar. A dismount may then be made by following the path of movement in reverse, i.e. by pushing up with the arms, bringing the knees well up towards the chest, dropping backwards on straight arms and, at the bottom of the swing, withdrawing the legs by passing the feet back under the bar and continuing into a underswing by extending back, hips and knees. Dismount at the end of the ensuing backward-swing.

SHORT DESCRIPTION OF EXERCISE: *Overgrasp hang: heave-swing: pike to bar and seat circle forwards to sitting.*

Teaching points: The whole movement must be smooth, uninterrupted and well timed. There is no time lag, as in the seat circle backwards, and the movement is more difficult to perform. Again, an assistant may help the pupil by pushing up on his seat or back on the uprise.

19. *Starting position: Toward Standing: Mount to Overgrasp hang.*
From this position perform a heave-underswing and at the end of the forward-swing, pike to bar, bringing the right leg under the bar. Then quickly crook it over the bar close to and outside the right hand. The back-swing is continued into and uprise with the left leg being swung as vigorously as possible backwards. At the same time the arms press-pull and flex, to bring the head and trunk up and over the bar. The pupil finishes in forward astride position on the bar. From this position the right leg may then be circled half-right so that the pupil is then in a front rest/support position, and a dismount may then be made by a drop-back undershoot to land with back to bar.

SHORT DESCRIPTION OF EXERCISE: *Overgrasp hang: heave-swing and single-leg acting upstart to forward astride sitting/support – knee outside hands. See exercise 20 of low bar work.*

Teaching points: The hands must be kept close together thus allowing the crooked leg to be placed on the bar as near to the body mid-line as is possible. This facilitates the rock-up or uprise to the desired position on top of the bar. The force of the free (left) backward swinging leg is most important in assisting the uprise. A supporter may, if necessary, ensure the success of the movement by grasping the pupil's ankle and swinging the leg in the required direction, at the same time giving some lift also.

20. *Starting position: Toward Standing: Mount to Over-grasp Hang with hands shoulder-width apart.*

This exercise is basically the same as the previous one the only difference being that the single-leg circle up is performed with the right leg *between* the hands, instead of *outside* the right hand. From the position reached the pupil may descend

FIG. 32. Single leg circle up to rest. *Note* leg in position before backswing commences.

by dropping backwards on straight arms, at the same time withdrawing the right leg. Then continue smoothly into an underswing and dismount at the end of the backward-swing. See *Fig. 32.*

SHORT DESCRIPTION OF EXERCISE: *Overgrasp hand – hands shoulder-width apart – heave-swing and single-leg circle up, knee between hands.*

21. *Starting position: Sitting on bar with knees close together, hands in Overgrasp.*

From this position the pupil pushes up with his arms and at the same time crooks his knees and pushes his seat backwards until the backs of the knees fit snugly over the bar. Without pause, he then releases his grasp of the bar, swings his arms straight up overhead, and commences a backward rotation suspended only by his crooked knees. At the same time as the arms are swung overhead the head is thrown quickly backwards and the hips extended – there must be no bend at all at the hips. At the end of the three-quarter backward circle a landing is made by straightening the knee joints and then quickly partially flexing the hips. See *Fig. 33.*

SHORT DESCRIPTION OF EXERCISE: *Sitting, knees together, hands in overgrasp outside of knees. Hollow-back backward rotation and hock-swing dismount.*

Teaching points: It is most important that there shall be no bend at the hips during the circle back, otherwise the seat will tend to lead the movement and there is then a real danger of the pupil coming off the bar. At best, the swing will be impeded and a poor style movement will inevitably result. The hip joints must be fully extended, the back well arched and the arms swung vigorously over head to give impetus to the movement. The timing of the knee extension at the end of the forward-swing is equally important as premature release could cause the pupil to land flat on his face. Very often a pupil will release or straighten one leg at a time – this leads to imbalance and a consequent dangerous landing. The teacher must be on the look out for this and it is always best to have a waist belt fitted to the pupil during the learning stages on the high bar. However, if the movement has already been mastered on the low bar there should be little danger for

FIG. 33. Hock swing dismount from sitting.

it is easier to perform this particular movement on the high
bar than it is on the low one. When a waist belt is used the
supporter – one on either side – grasp the side ropes on the
belt as high as possible with the near hand, winding the rope
a couple of turns around the hand as a precaution against the
rope slipping through the hand. The tail of the rope is then
grasped in the other hand but sufficient slack in the rope must
be left to ensure that the pupil's swing back is not hindered in
any way. The supporters may thus follow the pupil's path of
movement and ensure that a good landing is made by giving
some lift at the end of the forward-swing. This aid to safety
may later be dispensed with, but the movement must always
be spotted.

22. *Starting position: Mount to Overgrasp Hang with
hands shoulder-width apart.*
Perform a heave-swing and on a back-swing keep the body
vertical and by pressing down strongly with the arms, uprise
to rest position.

SHORT DESCRIPTION OF EXERCISE: *Overgrasp heave-swing and uprise to rest.*

Teaching points: Do not allow the body to fly out from the bar on the back-swing but keep it vertical. The downward pressure of the arms plus the impetus of the swing should be sufficient to enable the front rest position to be reached. Some help may be given the pupil when he is learning the movement by pushing up on his seat as he is on the uprise. Alternatively the pupil may wear a belt with ropes attached to each side; the supporters then stand on high apparatus on either side of the pupil holding the ropes. As the pupil uprises they can assist him to gain the rest position by lifting on the ropes. They must be careful however, to lift vertically and not pull the pupil in towards the bar. Still standing on high apparatus, the supporters may dispense with the ropes and by grasping his upper arm with the other on the uprise, they may lift him into a rest position. It is necessary to impress upon the pupil that on no account must the arms be bent when attempting the uprise; this kills the movement completely. See *Fig.* 34.

23. *Starting position: Toward Standing: Mount to Undergrasp Hang.*

Heave-swing and at the end of a forward-swing, when the feet are at peak height, pike to bar, i.e. swing the straight legs towards the bar – bring feet to bar. Then beat out and down with the straight legs and at the same time press down strongly with the arms, keeping the back slightly arched and the head well back. The beat of the legs gives 'lift' to the trunk and this, together with the downward pressing arms, should be sufficient to bring head and trunk up above the bar. As the legs swing backwards-upwards the arms pull the chest forward over the bar so that a rest position is reached.

SHORT DESCRIPTION OF EXERCISE: *Toward standing: mount to undergrasp hang and upstart to front rest.*

Teaching points: The undergrasp upstart is more difficult than the overgrasp one and care must be taken not to bend the arms during the leg beat and uprise otherwise the trunk is pulled in towards the bar, thus preventing rotation and effectively 'killing' the movement. The essentials of the skill

FIG. 34. Heave swing and uprise to rest. *Note* vertical position of
body on uprise and straight arms pressing down.

are good timing – *too much* swing is as bad as *too little* swing.
Again, some assistance may be given by supporters standing
on high apparatus, as described in exercise 22, and giving the
pupil some lift on the uprise by pulling up on ropes attached
to the pupil's waist belt.

The upstart is a very useful means of commencing advanced
sequences, such, for example, as a preliminary to giant forward or backward circles where the upstart may be followed
by a good throw up to handstand and a push away into a
giant circle. Again, a good example of using an upstart as a
lead up to a sequence is as follows: overgrasp heave-swing
and upstart to front rest followed immediately by a hip circle
backwards; finish the hip circle by dropping backwards on
straight arms – bringing toes to bar – and continue into an
underswing; dismount at the end of a back-swing with a
quarter-right/left turn.

24. *Starting position: Toward Standing: Mount to Under-grasp Front Support.*

From this position throw up into a handstand by first swinging the legs forward under the bar and then again vigorously backwards-upwards. This is not easy and the pupil may find that he has difficulty in achieving this. The hand balance is not held but the pupil, with his arms at full stretch, rotates forward, pushing strongly away with his arms. Without further effort he is able to perform a three-quarter forward circle and at the end of the swing he may dismount by pulling inwards with his arms and flexing his hips to bring his body to a vertical position. He then pushes away with his arms and lands facing the bar. Alternatively he may, at the end of the swing quickly change his hand grasp to overgrasp and continue swinging, dismounting then at the end of a forward- or backward-swing.

SHORT DESCRIPTION OF EXERCISE: *Undergrasp front rest: throw into a hand balance and immediate three-quarter circle forwards: dismount at end of backward- or forward-swing.*

Teaching points: When the pupil first attempts the throw up to hand balance he may be assisted in this by two supporters standing on high apparatus – one on each side, as already described. They may then grasp the pupil's upper arm with the near hand stabilising him, and with the other hand placed on the pupil's chest as he swings up to a hand balance they may give lift and forward rotation. They may also safeguard the pupil by maintaining the wrist grasp throughout the three-quarter circle, quickly changing the hand grasp from one hand to the other as the circle proceeds. Alternatively the pupil may be fitted with wrist straps which may be clipped on to the bar and which rotate around the bar as the pupil circles forward. Or again, instead of being clipped on to the bar the supporters may grasp the free end, changing hands, as already described, as the pupil circles forward.

Other devices may be used, e.g. overhead ropes and pulleys – the ropes are attached to a waist belt at one end and the other end passes through overhead pulleys. The advantage of this method is that one person, standing on the floor may safeguard the pupil. I think, however, that direct manual assistance is best at this stage of learning. Once the pupil has gained confidence and is used to this movement, he may then proceed to learn the full circle, returning again to the hand balance position on the bar. However, the final quarter circle is the most difficult part of the exercise and there are one or two important things to remember:

(a) as the body rises and reaches ten-to-twelve position, the wrists must be quickly twisted to bring the heels of the hands on top of the bar.

(b) Secondly, the arms are bent very slightly to pull the body-weight over the bar and to assist rotation.

When attempting the full circle for the first time, and in fact, for some considerable time afterwards, the supporters should use the wrist strap method to ensure the safety of the pupil. In addition to this, the supporters may assist the pupil on the return circle-up to hand balance by pressing up on his chest on the uprise. On completing the circle the pupil may either descend to front rest from the hand balance position or continue circling forward and finishing, as previously described, after a three-quarter forward circle.

This is a challenging and exhilarating exercise which demands a spirit of daring on the part of the learner and good coaching on the part of the teacher. There is no real reason why any average gymnast should not be able to perform the giant circle if he has the necessary courage and a strong enough desire to master it. The three-quarter circle is a necessary lead up to the full circles, i.e. giant circles which are now described.

25. *Starting position: Overgrasp Front Rest – thumbs around the bar.*

From this position the pupil throws up into a hand balance and without pause pushes away from the bar to the full extent of his arms, the object being to obtain sufficient momentum to complete a full reverse circle around the bar back to the original hand balance position. The first part is fairly easy and two supporters, standing on high apparatus on either side of the pupil, may assist him to get up to the hand balance position preparatory to attempting the circle. At the end of the three-quarter circle the pupil checks by pulling in with his arms and flexing at the hips to bring the body to a vertical position. A dismount may then be made by thrusting against the bar before releasing the hand grasp. Having got used to the sensation the pupil may next proceed to attempt the full circle and should go all out for it with supporters assisting as described, i.e. by grasping the pupil's wrists; changing hands as the pupil moves around the bar and by pulling on his upper arms assist him to get to a hand balance position on top of the bar again. In addition, the pupil should wear wrist straps which are clipped on to the bar and which rotate around the bar with him. Contrary to what might be thought, the straps do not get in the way and is the method by which, unassisted, I learnt the giant circles myself. The crucial stage of the circle is on the last quarter-circle when the extended body rises above the horizontal plane. The pupil must then, very quickly and smoothly, hollow out the back, throw his head well back and at the same time quickly twist his wrists in order to get the hands over the bar, a position from which he is then enabled to push up against the bar. If the wrist action is not correctly carried out and the wrists are kept flexed, or even straight, he cannot possibly finish the circle and, having got so far will then drop back down again. When this occurs he must fold up, bringing the head forward again and check the movement by semi-flexing the arms and shortening the lever. The supporters must watch for this and must assist in checking the return movement when failure to complete the full circle is apparent. The presence of the supporters, however, should ensure that the pupil achieves success. With practice he should subsequently be able to perform several such circles in succession and when this stage is reached he may then link the circles to other movements to make interesting and spectacular sequences.

The straps mentioned may be made at any saddlers and consist of a wrist strap about two inches wide, to which is attached a short leather thong – about five inches long – or a chain. The thong or chain is clipped on to the bar outside the hands by means of a large spring clip such as climbers use. This precaution gives pupils a feeling of safety and confidence – a fall during the learning stages can often deter a pupil permanently. Such a precaution also reduces the strain on the supporters who are still necessary of course. They feel that the pupil is not wholly dependent upon the strength of their grip.

SHORT DESCRIPTION OF EXERCISE: *Overgrasp front support: throw up to hand balance and three-quarter backward/ reverse circle.* See *Fig.* 35.

FIG. 35. Overgrasp backward giant circle.

26. *Starting position: Toward Standing.*

Spring to undergrasp hang and from an underswing upstart to hand balance proceeding straight away into a forward giant circle; when the circle is completed and the hand balance position is again reached, make a half-left turn, releasing the grasp of the right hand and swinging it over to re-grasp the bar. Both hands are now in overgrasp; without pause, continue circling in the opposite direction, i.e. backward circle. Finish in front rest position. See *Fig.* 36, showing forward giant circle.

SHORT DESCRIPTION OF EXERCISE: *Undergrasp hang and*

upstart to hand balance and giant circle forwards – half-left body turn changing grasp of the right hand to overgrasp and continue into a reverse or backward giant circle – finish in front support.

Teaching points: This sounds a formidable exercise and indeed when learning it, no wrists straps can be used. This, however, need not deter the performer who has already learnt both giant circles, for supporters can stand in and to some extent safeguard the movement. As a lead-up the pupil may perform a forward giant circle, make his half turn and then return to front rest or just carry on into a three-quarter circle. Once the change has been made, however, there is nothing to stop the whole movement being continued – this will largely be a matter for the individual to decide.

27. *Starting position: Toward Standing.*

Mount to overgrasp hang with hands shoulder-width apart. Perform a heave-swing and on the second or third forward-

FIG. 36. Undergrasp forward giant circle.

swing, when sufficient height has been attained, and the legs have swung up high above bar level, the hand grasp is released and the body rotates backwards as a long lever, i.e. a fly-away back somersault is performed and the performer lands with his back towards the bar. See *Fig. 37.*

SHORT DESCRIPTION OF EXERCISE: *Overgrasp hang: underswing followed by a fly-away back somersault to land with back towards bars.*

Teaching points: This is not a very difficult feat although there are some dangers implicit in it. The whole movement from start to finish may be safeguarded by means of two supporters standing one on each side of the pupil, who wears a waist belt with ropes attached. The supporters, by grasping

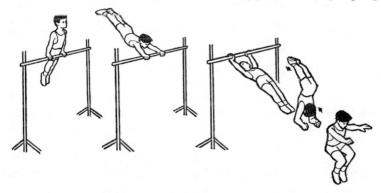

FIG. 37. Heave swing fly-away back somersault.

the rope, near the pupil's waist, firmly with the near hand and holding the tail of the rope in the other, may support and follow the whole movement throughout until a safe landing is made. It must be stressed that the mere release of the hand grasp when the legs are at peak height will not ensure that the somersault is made – for if there was no positive movement of the arms and trunk the pupil would possibly land flat on his back or even worse. In fact, as the legs swing up and backwards the back should be arched, and the head and arms swung backwards to assist backward rotation. There are two versions of this, i.e. a hollow back, back somersault or a tuck somersault in which the legs swing up and the hips sharply flexed (piked) as the head and trunk rotate backwards.

Because in the latter there is a more compact body-mass, rotation is easier and quicker. In both types however, the body is completely extended just before a landing is made.

Very often the movement may be practised over water if there are available roman rings or a high bar erected over water. The movement may also be practised out-of-doors over a sand-pit or similar soft landing.

EXAMPLES OF SEQUENCES ON THE HIGH BAR

1. *Overgrasp Hang:* Underswing and on back-swing squat through with the right leg and single-leg half-circle forward to forward astride on top of the bar (single-leg acting upstart). Half-left turn, quickly changing the relative position of the hands; drop-back immediately, withdrawing the left leg; short underswing and dismount with a half-right turn, on a backward swing.

2. *Overgrasp Hang:* Underswing and on the second forward-swing make a half-left turn changing over the grasp of the right hand; swing forward and then squat through with the left leg (i.e. bring the leg under the bar between the hands and crook the knee over the bar). Single-leg circle up to forward astride on top of the bar; make a half-left circle of the right leg with a half-left body-turn to front rest; drop-back with short underswing and dismount on the backward-swing with a quarter-left turn.

3. *Overgrasp Hang:* Heave underswing and on the second forward-swing squat through with both legs and circle up (forwards-upwards) to sit on top of the bar. Swing both legs forward and push off with hands to alight with back to bar.

4. *Overgrasp Hang:* Underswing and squat through with the right leg and single-leg circle up to forward astride on top of the bar. Half-right circle of left leg to sit on bar: seat circle backwards followed by a drop-back and squat out with both legs; continue into a short underswing followed by an upstart to front rest; hip circle backwards, again followed by a drop-back and underswing dismount to land with back to bar.

5. *Overgrasp Hang:* Heave underswing followed by an up-start; forward circle (roll) and then face-vault over bar (left or right), to land with side towards bar (side standing).

6. *Overgrasp Hang:* Underswing and back uprise followed by a short clear circle backwards; continuing into an under-underswing; dismount at the end of the back-swing with a quarter-left turn.

7. *Overgrasp Hang:* Underswing followed by a squat through with the right leg and single-leg half-circle forwards to forward astride on top of the bar. Mill circle backwards followed by a drop-back, at the same time withdrawing the right leg. Continue into an underswing and on the ensuing forward-swing flex at the waist to bring the feet towards the bar, at the same time parting the legs to wide astride and placing the heels against the back of the bar outside of the hands; on the next forward-swing perform a heel-swing dismount to land with back to bar.

8. *Overgrasp Hang:* Underswing and squat through with the right leg, crooking the knee over the bar. Ride up as high as possible on the forward-swing short of getting on top of the bar and then swinging back down again, perform a single-leg circle up backwards to forward astride position on top of the bar. Change hands to undergrasp and mill circle forward to finish on top of the bar again; half-right circle of left leg, at the same time making a half-right body-turn to front rest (hands now in overgrasp). Drop-back, at the same time keeping the legs straight and bringing the feet to the bar (pike to bar). Perform an underswing and upstart to rest followed immediately by a hip circle backwards; undershoot dismount.

9. *Undergrasp Hang:* Heave underswing and upstart to front rest followed by an immediate throw up into a hand balance – immediately push away into a three-quarter forward circle and, at the end of the back-swing, change hand grasp to overgrasp and swing forward, bringing feet to bar at end of forward-swing; squat through with both legs and perform a seat circle backwards to sit on top of the bar. Change

the right hand grasp to undergrasp at the same time extending the hips and making a half-right body-turn (taking the weight on to the right arm, and keeping head and trunk well over the bar), to front rest; immediate drop-back and pike to bar; short upstart to rest followed by a hip circle backwards, continuing into a drop-back undershoot dismount. Land with back to bars.

10. *Overgrasp Hang*: Underswing and on the second forward-swing make a half-right body-turn, at the same time swinging the left arm over to re-grasp the bar in overgrasp; swing forward and squat through with the right leg to circle up to forward astride sitting on top of the bar; make a half-right circle of the left leg, at the same time making a half-right body-turn to front rest; cast away backwards to a (throw back) underswing. At the end of the forward-swing, pike to bar, at the same time parting the legs to wide astride placing the backs of the heels against the back of the bar and perform a heel-swing dismount.

THE TRAMPETTE AS AN AID TO HORIZONTAL BAR WORK

A trampette is a very useful adjunct to bar work and may be used to give impetus when it is desired to perform swinging movements on the bar. It enables weaker boys to learn the rudiments of bar work, thereby stimulating interest and encouraging them to persevere. Without its aid such boys might not be able to perform a heave-swing which, of course, is basic to high bar performance.

For medium height bar work the edge of the trampette (near edge) should be about five feet from the plane of the uprights or, for the more advanced and daring performers, as much as six feet away. Pupils may then take off from the trampette following a running approach or, where there is not sufficient run-up, from a down jump off a suitable piece of apparatus, e.g. the top of a box horse.

Examples of exercises which may be performed in this way are:

1. With bar about six to seven feet high, leap to overgrasp

the bar, hands shoulder-width apart, so that you can just look over the bar. Drop-back on straight arms, at the same time piking to bar and perform an undershoot dismount. See *Fig.* 38.

FIG. 38. Heave tuck undershoot.

2. Leap to front support on the bar and immediate drop-back undershoot dismount. See *Plate* 16, facing page 81, showing leap to bar and drop-back undershoot dismount.

3. Leap to overgrasp the bar – hands shoulder-width apart and shoulders about level with the bar with body extended behind. Swing legs forwards-upwards, over the bar, at the same time hollowing out the back, throwing the head well back and twisting the wrists quickly back in order to get the heels of the hands on top of the bar. Finish in front support (upward circle to rest/support). From here, dismount by undershoot or by performing a forward-roll dismount.

4. Leap for the bar to front suport and perform an immediate hip circle backwards, continuing into an undershoot dismount.

5. Low or medium height bar: from a double take off on the trampette perform a piked overswing from the bar. This is most effective for display work, using two trampettes – one on either side of the bars. This and many of the skills described above may be performed in pairs with partners approaching from opposite sides of the bar. The exercises may be performed by pairs simultaneously or quickly alternately or, again, by two teams working 'in stream'. This work,

basically simple, looks extremely effective when well
d well timed. See *Plate* 17.

ERAL ADVICE CONCERNING BAR WORK

Beginners will probably have some difficulty in understanding some of the exercises but they should not be discouraged by this. Body positions, movements and the terminology must be learnt if progress is to be made. It will be found that the various terms used will become very familiar with constant use.

Group work is the best means of obtaining good results, and when three or four work together for a common benefit on the basis of mutual help, results are quickly forthcoming. Obviously it is not possible to give, in detail, directions for support and assistance in respect of all exercises but the following points and advice will be found most helpful:

Be particular about the bar – see that it is not rusty or rough and that it has no bits sticking to it. A rough bar will very quickly tear the skin off the palms of hands and such injuries are exceedingly painful and take a long time to heal. A piece of very fine emery cloth must be used to polish the bar, and it is best cleaned in a rotary fashion around the circumference, rather than rubbing the bar with long strokes along its length. When the latter is done, fine striations are left which will grip the skin and quickly peel it off. There is less likelihood of this occurring if the fine striations are around the bar not along it. A slippery bar – especially if wet from sweaty hands – is most dangerous and the bar must, therefore, often be cleaned and wiped over. In addition, gymnasts use a magnesium derivative which is rubbed on to the hands and is an effective precaution against hand injury and the likelihood of slipping off the bar. Also obtainable are hand-protectors – frequently used these days – which protect the hands from the abrasive effect of the bar. These too may be purchased from a sports shop or they may be made from lamp wick or webbing by cutting a piece which reaches from the centre of the middle finger to just below the wrist. A hole is then cut in one end of the wick, large enough for the finger to be thrust through easily. The hole may then be button hole stitched, to make a professional job of it, and tapes sewn on the other end. The tapes are tied around the wrist after the middle finger has been thrust through the hole in the other end. These are quite effective but the magnesium may still be used on the protectors to prevent the material reeving up on the bar. The protectors bought in the store are of soft leather and ideal for the purpose.

When it is intended not to use the bar for some time it must be cleaned and covered with a film of vaseline; some rags or material wrapped around the bar afterwards will help to keep the bar from rusting due to damp. It should then be stored in a dry place – preferably heated.

For outside work a galvanised bar is best as it does not rust. Such bars should be erected over a sand pit as a safety measure and also because this obviates the need for mattresses. If it is intended not to make an outside bar a fixture, then an ordinary indoor rig may be used by screwing ground anchors firmly into the ground and then attaching the guy wires to the anchors. As many horizontal bars have a short metal peg at the end of the upright for fitting into a socket in the floor of the gymnasium, ground plates about six inches square must be provided, for use on soft ground, with a central hole to receive the peg of the uprights. A further precaution is to drill a hole in each corner of the plates through which six-inch nails may be pushed into the ground to provide extra purchase.

Where bars are permanently fixed outside they should be concreted into the ground and have permanent guys attached.

Always watch the head and shoulders of the pupil and do not allow him to attempt a feat for which he has not prepared sufficiently well. Many accidents are due to poor preparation and insufficient practice of interval skills.

Long trousers should be worn for all kinds of bar work. These should be close fitting and should have elastic stirrups for slipping over the socks – these keep the trousers taut and prevent reeving. Baggy trousers are dangerous and a serious accident may be caused by inadvertently gripping the slack of a loose fitting pair of trousers between hand and bar. Specially made gymnastic tights or trousers may be purchased at sports shops, although a pair of tapered ski trousers fitted with elastic stirrups will be found to be ideal for general purposes.

FIVE

RING WORK

Although nowadays many schools have gymnasia equipped with rings the latter are generally used only for swinging on and very little serious gymnastic work is ever done on them. They thus have an extremely limited use and often, they are not used at all, as one may observe from the new appearance even some considerable time after they have been installed.

The unpopularity of this work may be attributed to the fact that one has to be very strong to perform even the simplest of skills on them – especially where one has to get into a rest position on the rings before commencing a movement. Few people apparently have the perseverance to keep on trying until they are sufficiently strong to learn the various exercises.

With young beginners it is best to commence with the rings just a little above head height so that the pupil may gain some drive from his legs instead of having to rely solely on the strength of his arms, as when the rings are set at full stretch height. As the pupil gains strength the rings may be raised so that more arm and shoulder strength must be used.

The exercises outlined in the following pages are designed to help pupils to master ringwork and although some may appear to be ridiculously simple they none-the-less demand a good degree of strength and control.

THE EXERCISES

1. With the rings at stretch height grasp the rings and perform the following:
(a) Pull up and bring the rings close in to the chest – hold for a moment and then lower again. Do this several times until the arms are tired. This is a pure strengthener of the arm flexors.
(b) Repeat the movement and, holding the position as before, push one ring out sideways by stretching the arm. Bring the ring back in again; repeat with the opposite arm.

Teaching point: Keep the ring in close to the chest.

2. Practise the previous two exercises, bringing the knees well up in front first and keeping them in position whilst carrying out the arm movements.

3. Grasp the rings and hang at full stretch of the arms. Now extend one leg well behind, arching the back strongly and pressing the head well back. Swing the free leg forwards-upwards overhead and follow it quickly with the other leg which thrusts strongly against the floor to give added impetus. As the legs swing overhead the trunk rotates backwards until an inverted position is reached, i.e. the extended body is supported by the arms with the head towards the floor and the feet pointing towards the ceiling. The arms should be close to the sides, legs together and toes well pointed. From this inverted position try the following simple movements:

(a) arch your back a little, press your head well back and keep the rings close to your sides. *Plate* 18, facing page 96, shows inverted hang position.

(b) From the previous position, flex slightly at the hips and bring your head forward to look at your toes; now pull with your arms to project your extended body upwards as high as possible without losing control, then stretch them again to lower your body-weight. *Fig.* 39, shows pike position from inverted hang.

(c) Fold at the waist and bring your feet slowly downwards your face, keeping your legs perfectly straight. This is the familiar pike position. Now stretch up again, i.e. extend the hips and straighten the back.

(d) Next, allow your extended body to fall slowly forwards-downwards; check the speed, and control the movement with the arm and shoulder muscles; as the body falls, bend your arms so that you finish in bent-arm hang; release hand grasp and land with give at knees and ankles.

4. Reach up and grasp the rings – bend the knees to keep the feet clear of the floor and hang to the full extent of the arms (full-arm hang). Now raise your knees and circle up to

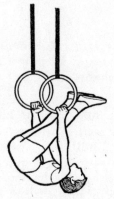

FIG. 39. Inverted hang to pike. *Note* eyes directed towards toes
preparatory to upstart.

place one foot in each ring; hollow out the back; extend the
knees and press your head well back. This position is known
as Bird's Nest. See *Plate* 19, facing page 96.

5. As for the previous exercise but withdraw one foot from
the ring and stretch the leg backwards; release the grasp of
the opposite hand and stretch this arm forwards. See *Plate* 20,
facing page 96.

6. Grasp the rings at stretch height and circle up and over,
allowing the body to rotate backwards as far as possible until
the feet almost touch the floor. Now circle back again. You
will be able to tell what your limit is so that you are able to
get back again but try to get a little further each time. This
exercise is known as 'skinning the cat'.

7. Perform the previous exercise again and when at the
limit of the movement cautiously release the grasp of one
hand. You will then spin around in a full circle at the end
of which you re-grasp with the free hand and finish in the
original starting position.

8. Grasp the rings and pull up to an inverted hang position, with the hips slightly bent. Pull up a little with both
arms and then straight away swing the right leg downwards

outside the right ring past the right hand, which is quickly
released for the leg to pass. As this is done, pull up strongly
with the left arm and re-grasp the right ring with the right
hand. Return to the starting position and repeat with the
left leg.

SHORT DESCRIPTION OF EXERCISE: *Inverted hang: Single-
leg cut and catch.*

9. *Full-Arm Hang:* Circle up to inverted hang, head forward a little and hips slightly bent. Pull up quickly with both
arms and at the same time cut outside the right ring with
both legs, as in the previous exercise, releasing the grasp of
the right hand and quickly re-grasping again. Finish in full-
arm hang.

SHORT DESCRIPTION OF EXERCISE: *Inverted hang: both legs
cut out and catch.*

10. *Full-Arm Hang:* Circle up to inverted hang. Swing the
straight legs downwards-forwards astride the rings, at the
same time pulling powerfully with the arms to pull the chest
in to the rings. The straight legs cut astride the rings, the
hand grasp being released for the legs to pass, and a landing
is made in a standing position.

SHORT DESCRIPTION OF EXERCISE: *Inverted hang: double-
leg cut off forward astride.*

Teaching point: A supporter must stand behind the pupil
when he attempts this exercise in case he does not have sufficient forward rotation to enable him to land on his feet.
There is a danger of the pupil landing with his weight falling
backwards and he could thus hurt himself. The supporter
standing behind, places his hands on the back of the pupil's
shoulders as he cuts-off, and by pushing forward imparts some
forward rotation, thus ensuring that the pupil lands on his
feet.

11. *Full-Arm Hang: Circle Up to Inverted Hang:* Look at
your toes and then allow the completely extended body to
swing forwards-downwards bending the arms and pulling the
chest into the rings as the body swings down. Without pause
swing the legs forwards-upwards astride the rings and, as the

legs almost touch the hands, the head and trunk are swung backwards and the hand grasp released. The whole body is quickly extended before the landing is made. See diagrams *Fig.* 40.

SHORT DESCRIPTION OF EXERCISE: *Double-leg cut-off backward astride or backward astride cut-off.*

Teaching point: A supporter should be standing by to push up on the pupil's chest as he releases the rings. This will ensure that he makes a safe landing. At first the pupil tends to land in a cramped up position but it must be impressed that as the legs swing back there must be vigorous extension of the trunk to assist backward rotation.

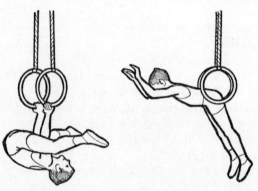

FIG. 40. Backward astride cut off dismount. *Note* hips are extended and body hollowed out as cut off is made.

12. *Starting position: Rings at Head height: Grasp Rings – palms of hands facing inwards.*

Swing one leg forwards-upwards quickly followed by the other, from a thrust against the floor. As the legs swing up overhead, pull vigorously with the arms and shoot the legs upwards and backwards and strongly arch the back. As the extended body begins to fall, push the arms out sideways to full stretch. This enables the head of the humerus to make a complete rotation in its socket and the body rotation continues to complete a full backward circle. This movement is known as a back dislocation and the falling body is checked by pulling in with the arms as the dislocation is completed.

SHORT DESCRIPTION OF EXERCISE: *Grasp rings at head height: backward dislocation.*

Teaching points: A supporter may assist the pupil as he attempts the shoot-up between the ropes by pushing up on his shoulders, thus ensuring that the pupil gains sufficient height to complete the dislocation successfully. If the arms are not pushed out sideways and if the body is not sufficiently elevated, serious hurt may result by the arms locking and causing some possible damage to the shoulder joint.

13. The above movement may also be performed in a forward direction and the starting position is the same. This movement is known as forward dislocation. Mount to inverted hang and then allow the body to fall or swing forwards-downwards. At the bottom of the swing, tuck the chin on to the chest and curl up by picking the knees well up and rounding the back. At the same time pull strongly with the arms and then push them out sideways as the tucked-up body rotates into a forward-roll which is completed when the original starting position is reached. Again, at the end of the roll, the movement is checked by pulling in with the arms.

SHORT DESCRIPTION OF EXERCISE: *Hanging-inward grasp: mount to inverted hang; swing forwards-downwards and perform a forward dislocation.*

Teaching points: Before attempting the movement from a full-arm hang it is best to have the rings at below head height and then jump into the forward dislocation. This gives the pupil some idea of what is required before he attempts the dislocation from the full-arm hang with his feet clear of the floor.

14. *Starting position: With the rings at head height, grasp them and mount up to Inverted Hang.*

From this position, bring the head slightly forward so that you can see your toes, and bend the hips slightly. Next, pike sharply to bring the straight legs down towards your chest and then immediately beat out and down with the legs; at the same time press down with the arms to elevate the head and chest. The beat of the legs plus the press-pull of the arms should be sufficient to enable you to get to a rest position on the rings. *Fig.* 41 shows upstart to rest.

SHORT DESCRIPTION OF EXERCISE: *Mount to inverted hang and upstart to rest.*

Teaching points: Assist the pupil to get to a rest position by pushing up on his back as he attempts to upstart to rest. Beginners usually manage to get to a bent-arm rest position only, but later, with a great deal of practice, they will be able to achieve an upstart with only a slight bending of the elbows.

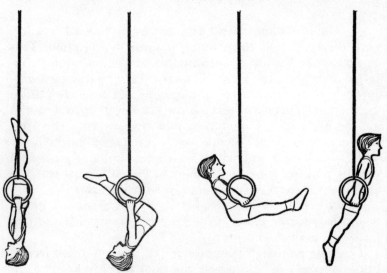

FIG. 41. Inverted hang, pike and upstart to rest. *Note* beat out with straight legs and press pull with arms.

As with all such upstarting movements good timing is the secret of success and the teacher/supporter may help with this by giving vocal commands or executives, i.e. with the pupil in inverted hang he will command: 'Down . . . and . . . Beat!' The direction 'Down' coincides with the movement to pike position, followed by a slight pause and then the executive 'Beat!' At the same time as the pupil beats in response to the command, the teacher/supporter gives manual assistance and guidance as described.

When, later, the pupil is able to upstart to rest with straight arms, he should be instructed to bend his elbows slightly as he reaches rest position, at the same time turning the rings inwards a little. Thus, the partly flexed elbows will contact the ropes and prevent the pupil possibly passing straight forward between the ropes.

15. The foregoing exercise was a *forward* upstart to rest but there is also a *reverse* upstart to rest. At least, this is the name given to what is really a circle up to rest, as done on the horizontal bar. In the case of rings, however, there is no bar to circle over, which makes the whole feat much more difficult.

Starting position: With the rings at head height, so that some drive may be obtained from the floor, grasp the rings with a false or overgrasp, i.e. the inner borders of the wrists are placed on the rings and the wrists are then fully flexed to grasp them – the palms of the hands facing downwards. It is easier to grasp in this way if the elbows are partly flexed but, even so, it is not a very comfortable position. The reason for grasping the rings in this way is so that the performer can pull-push into a rest position on the rings. He could not possibly do this if he hung from the rings with an ordinary grasp, for he must have the heels of his hands above the base of the ring before he can push up to rest.

The first part of the movement is very similar to the back dislocation previously described, i.e. the legs are swung vigorously forwards-upwards, either from a single or double footed take-off, and at peak height, coinciding with a vigorous pull-push of the arms, the hips are vigorously extended to shoot the legs upwards and backwards between the ropes. The momentum of the leg swing and hip extension plus the pull-push of the arms should be enough to bring head and shoulders above hand level and, as this point is reached, the hands turn the rings quickly outwards in order to bring the hands into a position from which the push-up can be made. The rings are kept close in to the sides of the body and the pupil may finish in a short-arm balance position or allow the body to swing down to a front rest position.

SHORT DESCRIPTION OF EXERCISE: *False grasp; reverse upstart or circle up to short-arm balance or rest.*

Teaching points: This is not a very easy movement to teach but once the pupil has a good mental image of what is required and has the necessary strength to perform the movement he should not take too long to learn it with assistance from a supporter. The latter may help by pushing up on the pupil's shoulders as he attempts the hip extension and leg shoot. This is the crucial point where success or failure is decided and 'lift' at this point will enable the pupil to complete the movement and thus gain the feel of it.

16. *Starting position: Adjust the rings to Head height and take a False Grasp as described in the previous exercise.*

Now pull strongly with the arms, keeping the elbows pointing obliquely forwards, and bring the rings in to the shoulders. Without pause, turn the wrists and rings outwards, at the same time bringing the chest forward between the rings, and pull-push up to rest position.

SHORT DESCRIPTION OF EXERCISE: *False grasp-pull up to rest position on rings. Plate* 21 (facing page 96), shows support/rest position on rings. Note arms locked against ropes for stability.

Teaching points: This exercise demands a great deal of strength and the pupil may be assisted initially by a supporter standing behind him and grasping his waist with his hands. As the pupil attempts the pull-up the supporter gives some 'lift', enabling the pupil to reach the rest position. The pupil may also set the rings low – about head height – and by jumping and pulling simultaneously get to a bent-arm rest on the rings. He may then attempt to push up to rest, but will probably need some assistance with this because of the tendency of the rings to move outwards as the pupil pushes up. The rest position itself is an unstable one for the beginner and it is best to tell the pupil to bring the rings close to his sides or alternatively to place the rings behind the back/buttocks and arching the back slightly to maintain balance.

Beginners should be told to flex the hips – swinging the legs forward when pulling up – and extending the hips again when pushing up to rest. This hip action helps considerably.

17. *Starting position: Rings at Head height – False Grasp.*
Pull up to rest and then bring the knees well up towards the chest. Elevate the hips and rotate forwards, keeping the

body well tucked up, and perform a forward roll to hang, extending the arms slowly and uncurling the body as the descent is made. *Plate* 22, facing page 97, shows the forward circle dismount.

SHORT DESCRIPTION OF EXERCISE: *False grasp-hang. Pull up to rest and tuck forward-roll dismount.*

Teaching point: Assist the pupil to get to the rest position, and stand by ready to check too rapid descent as the forward-roll is made. This is not too difficult an exercise to master but it needs a little nerve at first.

18. *Starting position: Take up a False Grasp of the Rings.*

Pull up to rest, pick the knees up in front and attempt a curl up into a short-arm balance, taking care to turn the rings slightly inwards and bending the arms so that they can be braced against the ropes. Braced in this way most pupils can make a reasonable initial attempt to get to the short-arm balance position.

When the balance position can be held, turn the rings outwards and lower into an inverted hang. Lower the legs forwards-downwards and dismount to stand.

SHORT DESCRIPTION OF EXERCISE: *False grasp: pull up to rest; mount up to a short-arm balance and dismount through inverted hang.*

Teaching points: When the pupil attempts the balance movement, initially, have the rings sufficiently low so that a supporter can reach up and stabilise the pupil in position as well as assist him into the balance. The supporter may also take some of the pupil's weight as he lowers into the inverted hang position.

19. *Starting position: False Grasp-pull up to Rest.*

From this position place the rings behind the body just below the buttocks – backs of the hands to the buttocks. Now arch the back, press the head well back and lean backwards keeping the hands tight against the buttocks and pivot or rotate backwards over the hands until the inverted hang position is reached. Descend or dismount by lowering the legs forwards or backwards or finish the movement by using any of the leg cut-offs, already described. *Plate* 23, facing page 97, shows backward circle to inverted hang or dismount. Note support.

SHORT DESCRIPTION OF EXERCISE: *False grasp-pull up to rest position. Place rings behind and backward circle dismount through inverted hang.*

Teaching points: Assist the pupil to rotate backwards by giving some lift – applied to the underpart of one of his thighs. At the same time place the other hand under his shoulder to take some of his weight as he approaches the inverted hang position. This is all that is required in this exercise.

20. *Starting position: Take a False Grasp and pull up to Rest Position.*

Now turn the rings slightly inwards, bracing the forearms against the ropes, and press up to a hand balance. Hold the balance and then lower to a short-arm balance, still keeping the arms braced as described, and then into an inverted hang position. From here, pike and upstart to rest and forward circle dismount.

SHORT DESCRIPTION OF EXERCISE: *From rest position press up to a full-arm balance and descend through short-arm balance to inverted hang. Pike upstart to rest and forward-roll dismount.*

Teaching points: Have the rings at chest height at first so that the pupil may be supported and assisted into the hand balance position. At such height the supporter may then stabilise the pupil in position and watch him through his descent to inverted hang via short-arm balance. He can then provide support as required.

SWINGING MOVEMENTS WITH RINGS AT STRETCH HEIGHT

In order to commence a swing on the rings, grasp them and take a couple of short running steps backwards, followed by a little upward-jump and semi-flexing the arms. Swing forward in this position, keeping the arms flexed in order to keep the feet off the floor. At the bottom of the swing give a smart one-two push-away with the feet and swing the legs well up in front. Follow this by vigorously extending hips and arms prior to the commencement of the return swing. Again, at the bottom of the swing, give a one-two push off with the feet and so on until a good swing is reached.

Now, on the backward-swing, lift the legs overhead to a piked position – bending the knees in order to do this if necessary – and continue swinging in the piked position. At the end of each forward- and backward-swing slightly extend and flex the hips to give a kind of pumping action with the straight legs. This action has the effect of increasing the swing. Finally, after several swings, dismount by unfolding or extending from the piked position at the end of a forward-swing, allowing the body to swing out to the full extent of the arms. Dismount with a vertical uprise at the end of the back-swing, i.e. with the body in a vertical position.

Other swinging movements are:

1. Swinging in the hang position with a half-right/left turn at the end of the forward-swing to face in the opposite direction.

The turn is made by swinging the body around and crossing the arms and ropes. At the end of the swing the body turns to face the original direction – the ropes being uncrossed again as the turn is made.

2. Swinging with a half-right/left turn at the end of the back-swing.

3. Swing in a hanging position and then lift legs up to an inverted pike position. Increase the range of the swing by making small pumping movements of the legs, as already described. Continue by extending the hips and swinging the legs downwards at the end of a forward-swing and lifting to a pike position at the end of the backward-swing. Repeat this continuously several times bending the knees when lifting on the back-swing and extending them on the forward-swing.

This is an extremely demanding exercise and requires strong abdominal and hip flexors.

4. Swing in a piked position and at the end of a back-swing, upstart to rest.

The upstart must be carried out at precisely the right moment, just as the end of the back-swing is reached. The essence of the movement is good timing and if the arms are bent with the elbows pointing out sideways across the ropes, there is little danger of upstarting right through them. Should this happen it could be very dangerous. The learner should therefore make a few tentative movements before deciding to go all out for it.

Later, the arms may be kept fairly straight but the elbows should still be kept slightly turned outwards as a safeguard. In the support position, keep the arms against the ropes and try swinging in this position. The following dismounts may then be made according to choice:

(a) At the end of a forward-swing allow the legs to swing up in front and then body shoot outwards to the full extent of the arms. Swing back at arm's length and dismount at the end of the back-swing.

(b) In the rest position – at the end of the back-swing, swing the legs up behind and execute a body-shoot backwards to the full extent of the arms. Continue the body-swing forward and dismount at the end of the ensuing back-swing.

(c) Swinging in rest position – towards the end of a forward-swing, pick the knees well up, elevate the seat and perform a forward-roll to continue into a hanging-swing. The extension of the body after or following on the roll must coincide with the end of the forward-swing. Continue the swing and dismount at the end of the back-swing.

5. Swinging Crow's Nest: Bring the knees up at the end of a forward-swing and place a foot in each ring. Still swinging, hollow out the back to a nest position. Roll out of the position at the end of a forward-swing by rounding the back, withdrawing the feet and opening out to swing in a full-arm hang position. Dismount at the end of the next back-swing.

6. Swing and lift up to inverted pike position at the end of a back-swing. Again, at the end of a back-swing, cut outside the right ring with the right leg, releasing the hand grasp on that side and quickly re-grasping again after the leg has

passed. When making the cut and releasing the hand-grasp, the opposite arm should pull towards that side until the re-grasp is effected, when the arm may be extended again.

The movement should be practised at first with a small swing and with the rings adjusted to head height.

SHORT DESCRIPTION OF EXERCISE: *Swinging: single-leg cut-out at end of back-swing.*

7. Swing in an inverted pike position and at the end of a back-swing, pull up with the arms and at the same time cut forward astride with the legs outside the rings. As the legs almost touch the hands, the hand-grasp is released for the legs to pass and the pupil lands in a standing position on the floor. *Plate* 24, facing page 97, shows forward astride cut-off at end of back-swing. Note supporter.

SHORT DESCRIPTION OF EXERCISE: *Pike swing and forward astride cut-off, dismount at end of back-swing.*

Teaching points: It is necessary to have a supporter stand-ing behind. As the cut-off is made, the supporter places his hands on the pupil's shoulders and pushes upwards, thus en-suring that the pupil does not rotate backwards and fall on to his back. Forward rotation is ensured by the pupil pulling up with his arms at the same time as he cuts downward astride with his straight legs.

8. With the rings at a little above head height, get a good swing in the hang position and at the end of a forward-swing, swing the straight legs forwards, upwards and backwards astride the ropes. As the legs cut astride the ropes the hips are vigorously extended and the back hollowed out before a landing is made. Again, as the legs cut astride the arms pull up strongly to impart upward movement to the head and shoulders as the legs swing backwards.

SHORT DESCRIPTION OF EXERCISE: *Full-arm swing followed by a backward astride cut-off at end of forward-swing.*

Teaching points: This swinging cut-off is much easier than the one on the stationary rings. Because of the height attained not a great deal of momentum is required; beginners must be careful not to be too vigorous at first. The difficulty is in orientating oneself at the end of the swing but a few practice cut-offs with a supporter standing in to 'spot' the movement soon enables the pupil to adjust.

When standing in to safeguard, the supporter must stand at the point where the pupil is going to attempt his cut-off. He can then place a hand on the pupil's chest to give him support should he have rotated insufficiently. Equally, the supporter must be on his guard and watch for too much backward rotation with the pupil landing on his back, but this is not usual. Sometimes the pupil will baulk and perhaps release the grasp of one hand only; the supporter must watch for this and be ready for any emergency. Start with the rings at head height first but remember that the lower the rings the harder it is to perform the cut-off.

9. Swing on the rings at full-arm stretch and at the end of the forward-swing uprise into rest. This movement is similar to an upstart except that the hip flexion and leg beat is much smaller. The heave up to rest is made as the legs swing forward from a preceding swing-back and are then checked to coincide with the arm heave, before being swung back again as the rest position is reached.

Coinciding or quickly following on the arm-heave, the rings are brought in close to the sides of the chest and then turned outwards to bring the hands on top of the ring. The press up to rest follows. See *Fig.* 42.

SHORT DESCRIPTION OF EXERCISE: *Swinging uprise at end of forward-swing*.

Teaching points: From the back end of the swing as the body swings down, the hips are flexed and the legs swung forward; the legs are again swung back at the bottom of the swing and then quickly forward again. The forward-swing is sharply checked and coincides with the press-pull of the arms; the legs then beat backwards to give lift to the trunk thus enabling the pupil to gain a rest position on the rings.

The leg movement may then be analysed as swing forward on down-swing; back at bottom of swing, forward again on the forward-swing as the arms press strongly – check and backward-swing as the arms press up to rest.

With practice the uprise may be done with fairly straight arms.

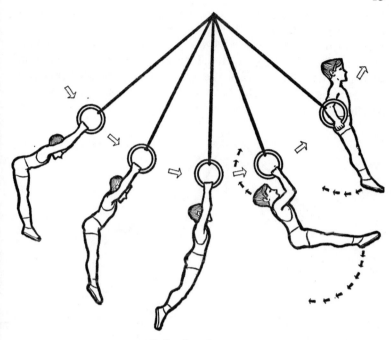

FIG. 42. Swinging forward uprise.

10. Swing with arms at full stretch and at the end of the back-swing, back-uprise into rest. On the back-swing the body is kept almost vertical with semi-flexed hips – as on the horizontal bar. On the uprise the arms press down strongly as the legs beat back. The beat, plus the arm press, should be sufficient to enable the pupil to get to a rest position on the rings.

SHORT DESCRIPTION OF EXERCISE: *Swinging back uprise to rest. See Fig. 43.*

Teaching points: Brace the arms against the ropes when swinging in the rest position – this is a safety precaution to prevent one slipping or swinging forward between the ropes.

11. Swing at full arms' stretch and upstart to rest at the end of the back swing. The upstart has already been described on the stationary rings and the swinging upstart is really much easier to perform.

From swinging, lift the legs up to pike position at the end of the back-swing. Swing forward in this position and at the end of the ensuing back-swing upstart to rest. Brace the arms against the ropes and swing in this position. At the end of the forward-swing pick the knees up, round the back and roll-out – extending the body fully as the end of the swing is reached.

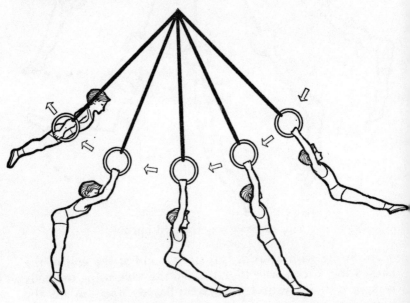

FIG. 43. Swinging back uprise to rest. *Note* use hip swing and leg beat to give updrive.

SHORT DESCRIPTION OF EXERCISE: *Full-arm swing to pike-swing and upstart to rest at end of back-swing. Roll-out into full-arm swing and dismount at end of back-swing.*

Teaching points: The danger is in upstarting right through the ropes but if due caution is exercised and the elbows kept pointing out from the sides across the ropes as the upstart is attempted, this danger is reduced. Of course the pupil must already have mastered the upstart on stationary rings before attempting the swinging upstart. It is not really a difficult movement and again good timing is the important factor.

The foregoing should be sufficient to give the beginner a good grounding on ring work. There are many more advanced exercises, e.g. forward dislocation at the end of a forward-swing and backward dislocation at the end of a back-swing but a great deal of practice is required before attempting these advanced movements.

POINTS OF GENERAL INTEREST

1. For beginners, the rings should be set at such a height that they can easily place the inside of their wrists on the rings, when standing on the tips of their toes. This will enable them to gain some drive from the floor for the more difficult movements and those demanding great arm strength.

2. A line of mats should be placed on the floor under the rings and should extend for the full length of the swing, at least.

3. Rings must not be used when the hands are sweaty – a dusting chalk or magnesia should be used.

4. It is pleasant to swing on the rings but do not hang on too long. It is surprising how easily the fingers lose their grip when fatigue creeps on.

5. It is best to always have a partner working with you, for a little assistance from him at the right time is often all that is needed to achieve success. Self help and mutual aid are vital in all gymnastic work.

6. For more advanced pupils the rings may be set much higher – about eight feet high – and then a partner will be needed in order to push you and so provide a swing. He does this by standing behind and placing his hands on your hips. He then runs forward, pushing you forward at the same time, and at the end of his run, as you rise above him he gives one last vigorous push and continues running forward under you. From this initial swing you may then increase your swing greatly by the means already described, i.e. 'pumping' the legs whilst in a piked position on the rings.

Swinging on the rings can be quite dangerous and a mis-timed leg beat or a movement performed at the wrong part of the swing could have disastrous results. On the other hand there is scarcely any other work which can be quite as exhilarating, enjoyable and physically beneficial, for this work is almost unparalleled for its effect in developing arms and the upper parts of the body – the legs are very little used. In this respect the rings have similar physical effects to the horizontal and parallel bars but this need not cause too much concern for, generally speaking, we use our legs a great deal more than we use our arms. Today, we are inclined still more to participate in recreative activities which make very little demand upon the musculature of the upper body. Natural swinging and climbing movements – at least in so far as schools' physical education goes – are rarely used in modern P.E. and the accent appears to be more on games, rather than on gymnastic exercises.

SIX

POMMEL HORSE SKILLS

When one sees the truly wonderful performances of the Olympic gymnasts on the pommel horse, one cannot but marvel at the remarkable dexterity, control and consummate skill which they display.

To the uninformed onlooker, the rhythmical, flowing ease with which the highly involved, continuative movements are performed belies the tremendous muscle fitness and physical strength that are required. It is not until one attempts even the simplest type of leg circle that one can begin to assess the qualities needed for such work.

It is true to say, however, that top performers on the pommel horse, as well as on other pieces of Olympic apparatus, are compact, powerful individuals, not generally tall, but with excellently developed upper body musculature tapering down to slimmer but well muscled legs. Olympic gymnasts are not usually large, heavily built men. There are exceptions, of course, but the best performers are more often as described.

This fact need not discourage aspirants of all types of build, for anyone can enjoy this type of gymnastics, especially if they start young. Then, physical strength and development keeps pace with growth, and young people grow up with the ability to handle their own body-weight with ease. It is the under-developed, flabby individual who has never practised such exercises who finds this work beyond his powers at first. He must therefore undertake a rigorous course of training in order to condition himself to the demands of Olympic gymnastic work.

Because of a possible deformative effect, young pupils should not attempt long continuative exercises on the pommel horse. Their work should consist of short, simple skills such as are now described:

THE EXERCISES

1. *Starting position: Toward Standing.*
Run forward and, grasping the pommels, vault to stand

astride them, keeping the legs straight and elevating the hips in order to place the feet on the horse. Now, release the hand grasp and stand erect. Dismount with one leg swinging forwards and land with give at ankles, knees and hips.

SHORT DESCRIPTION OF EXERCISE: *Stand facing the side of horse; run forward and, grasping pommels, vault to astride standing. Dismount with single leg swinging forward.*

Teaching point: Stress that elevation of the hips, i.e. bouncing the hips well above shoulder level, is essential to accomplish this exercise correctly. When the pupil attempts the movement first, have a supporter standing in facing him as he vaults in case he tips forward. The supporter may prevent this happening by placing his hands – straight arms – on the pupil's shoulders before he stands erect. Later, increase the height of the horse and use a trampette for the take-off. This is a more interesting and stimulating variation.

2. *Starting position: Toward Standing.*

Run forward, grasp the pommels, and perform an astride-vault over the right pommel, the left leg being bent and passing between the pommels whilst the right leg is kept fairly straight and passes over the right pommel. The grasp of the right hand is released for the right leg to pass whilst the body-weight is transferred on to the left arm. Following the right leg circle the right hand does not re-grasp the pommel but a quarter-left body turn is made, pivoting on the left arm. A landing is made with the left side of the body towards the apparatus (side standing), with the left hand still grasping the left pommel.

SHORT DESCRIPTION OF EXERCISE: *Toward standing; run forward to grasp pommels and astride-vault over right pommel (wolf-vault) with a quarter-left turn to land in side standing with left side towards horse.*

Teaching points: Instruct the pupil to lean well over on to the supporting arm as the right leg circle is made. Push away strongly with the right arm and then swing the arm vigorously around to the left in order to assist the left turn. The left arm (supporting arm) must be kept quite straight as the body pivots on it.

3. *Starting position: Toward Standing.*

Run forward and in one smooth movement grasp the pommels and perform an astride-vault to land on the far side of the horse with back towards it.

SHORT DESCRIPTION OF EXERCISE: *With a running approach astride-vault clear over pommels.*

Teaching points: The main points here are that the pupil must elevate his hips sufficiently to enable the straight legs to clear the apparatus. As the legs move forward astride the horse, the arms must thrust down very vigorously to push the head and trunk upwards and so offset the tendency to forward rotation through the elevation of the hips. Following the push away of the arms the hands are released and then swung forwards. A landing is made with the back towards the apparatus. As previously mentioned the landing shock must be received by bending ankle, knee and hip joints.

4. *Starting position: Toward Standing.*

Run forward and grasping the pommels astride-vault over the right pommel, quickly re-grasping with the right hand after the leg has passed over the right pommel. Finish sitting on the horse between the pommels.

SHORT DESCRIPTION OF EXERCISE: *Toward standing: astride-vault over right pommel to sit between pommels.*

Teaching points: As for exercise 2, lean weight over on to left arm as the right leg circles over pommel.

5. *Starting position: Toward Standing.*

Run forward, grasp the pommels and spring to front support, i.e. weight well over the hands; body inclined well forward with front of thighs resting against the horse. This should be a good looking position with arms straight, body nicely extended, toes pointed and chin tucked in a little. Dismount from this position by swinging the legs backwards and at the same time thrusting away with both arms. Retain the grasp of the pommels as the landing is made, with a slight bending of the lower body joints. Finish standing facing the horse. *Fig.* 44 shows front support or front leaning thigh rest. Note weight well over hands.

SHORT DESCRIPTION OF EXERCISE: *Toward standing: run*

forward, grasp pommels and mount to front support. Dismount with legs swinging backwards.

Teaching points: Check for good body position as described. Flex hips a little before back-swing of legs.

FIG. 44. Front support or front leaning thigh rest. *Note* weight over hands.

6. *Starting position: Toward Standing.*

Run forward, grasp pommels and mount to front support, at the same time leaning the weight on to the right arm. Swing the left leg forward over the left pommel, releasing the grasp of the left hand momentarily for the leg to pass and then quickly re-grasping. Continue this movement by swinging the body sideways to the right, transferring the weight on to the left arm, and circle the right leg forward over the right pommel, again releasing the grasp of the right hand for the leg to pass and then quickly re-grasping. Finish in back support and then dismount by swinging both legs forward, at the same time pushing off with the arms. Land with the back towards the apparatus.

SHORT DESCRIPTION OF EXERCISE: *With a short run grasp pommels and spring to front rest circling left leg forward over left pommel; circle right leg over right pommel to finish in back rest and dismount with legs swinging forward. Fig. 45 shows back rest/support position.*

Teaching points: Immediately the spring to front rest is made the left leg commences its right circle over the left pommel, i.e. it is one smooth movement and there is no pause in front rest before circling the leg over. In fact the leg commences its forward circle from the moment of take-off. Initially, allow the pupil to stop in back rest before circling the right leg over the pommel to the left but, later, all movements should flow one into the other smoothly and without check.

Lateral body-swings should take place from the shoulders and hips and should be loose and relaxed. When leg circles or half circles are being practised the body must lean to the opposite side to that on which the circles are being made. A rhythmical lateral body swing must be also practised.

FIG. 45. Back support. *Note* weight over hands, straight arms.

7. *Starting position: Toward Standing.*

Walk quickly forward, grasp the pommels and without any pause perform an astride cut-in and catch. Finish sitting on the horse, between the pommels, re-grasping with both hands as the sitting position is taken. Later, attempt the cut-in to finish in back support.

SHORT DESCRIPTION ON EXERCISE: *Astride cut-in to sit between the pommels.*

Teaching points: First practise to astride standing, i.e. feet astride the pommels. Then, with a supporter grasping the waist from behind and giving 'lift', attempt the whole movement. It is not really so hard as it appears at first sight. The supporter may either grasp a waist-belt centrally behind and walk forward with the pupil or, the feat may be attempted from a standing position with the supporter lifting with both hands. Another good method is to set the horse really high and use a trampette to gain impetus. The horse should be about mid chest height when the pupil is standing on the trampette facing it. Thus the pupil not only obtains a good lift from the trampette but is able to get a good downward thrust with the arms in order to elevate the trunk and thus prevent forward rotation.

8. *Starting position: Toward Standing.*

Stand close to the horse and grasp the left pommel with the right hand reverse in overgrasp. Place the left hand on the end of the horse and then vault to support position, taking almost all the body-weight on to the right arm. At the same time make a half-left body-turn to grasp the free pommel with the left hand and finish in back support. Now pick both knees up high and pass the legs backwards over the horse between the pommels. Then dismount by extending the hips and shooting the legs backwards, at the same time pushing strongly away with the arms.

SHORT DESCRIPTION OF EXERCISE: *Stand facing the left end of horse and grasp the left pommel with the right hand in reverse overgrasp, i.e. back of hand towards body, and left hand on end of horse. Spring with a half-left turn to back support; dismount with backward shoot of legs over horse between pommels.*

Teaching points: In taking up the grasp of the right hand the elbow is turned outwards and the hand turned inwards as far as possible so that the palm of the hand faces away from the body. As the spring to support is made, straighten the right arm and pivot around on it to the left; the left arm is swung around to the right to assist the body turn before it grasps the free pommel. This is not a difficult exercise but the initial hand grasp is an awkward one.

9. *Starting position: Toward Standing.*

Grasp the pommels and, with a spring, half-left circle of both legs over the right pommel and finish the movement in back support. From this position half-left circle of left leg over left pommel followed by half-right circle of right leg over right pommel – finish in front support. Dismount with legs swinging backwards and pushing away with the arms.

SHORT DESCRIPTION OF EXERCISE: *Toward Standing: grasp pommels and half-left circle of both legs over right pommel: half-left circle left leg over left pommel; half-right circle of right leg over right pommel to finish in front rest: dismount with legs swinging backwards.*

Teaching points: The whole exercise must be performed rhythmically in continuous movement from start to finish.

10. *Starting position: Toward Standing.*

Grasp pommels and vault to front support. Half-right circle left leg over left pommel, releasing the grasp of the left hand for the leg to pass and then re-grasping. From this position – forward astride rest, Fig. 46 – practise a lateral body swing, as described previously, with free movement from shoulders and hips and transferring weight alternately from one arm to the other, i.e. as legs swing up to the left, lean over to the right and *vice-versa.* Now, on a left side swing, half-left circle of the left leg over the left pommel. Again, on the return swing to the right, swing the right leg forward over the right

FIG. 46. Forward or front astride rest.

pommel (half-left circle of right leg). On the return body-swing to the right, half-right circle of the right leg over the right pommel to finish in support position. Dismount with legs swinging backwards.

SHORT DESCRIPTION OF EXERCISE: *Toward standing: vault to front support; half-right circle of left leg; half-left circle of left leg; half-left circle of right leg; half-right circle of right leg to finish in support position. Dismount with legs swinging backwards.*

Teaching points: Keep the body swing going continuously and freely. Assist the swing by pushing away alternately with the arms – keeping them straight all the while. A great deal of practice is needed to become really expert at this type of exercise.

11. *Starting position: Toward Standing.*

Grasp the pommels and perform a face-vault to the left to sit astride the horse, between the pommels. The grasp of the left hand must be quickly released for the body to pass, and transferred to the other pommel alongside the right hand. You should now be facing along the length of the horse with both hands grasping the pommel, in front. Now push up with both arms, to take the full body-weight, rock forward over the hands and, swinging the legs well up behind, dismount to the left to finish in side standing, right hand grasping the pommel.

FIG. 47. Astride rest.

SHORT DESCRIPTION OF EXERCISE: *Toward standing: grasp pommels and face-vault left to astride sitting between the pommels. Change to support, taking weight fully on to arms and rocking body-weight forward over hands, swing legs up behind and face-vault left to finish in side standing. Fig. 47 shows astride rest.*

Teaching points: Do not release grasp of the left hand until the legs have been well elevated, then quickly transfer alongside right hand in order to check the downward swing. When rocking the weight forward to complete the face-vault from support, the arms must be bent a little in order to get a good rock-up of the hips and legs; once they have been elevated then the arms are straightened as they push off for the dismount.

12. *Starting position: Toward Standing.*

Grasp pommels and spring to support position, at the same time making a quarter-left body-turn, and swinging the right leg forward over the end of the horse. You will now be astride the horse with most of the body-weight supported on the right arm – the left hand remains on the left pommel. From this position, rock the body-weight forward and swing the legs well up behind so that a horizontal position of the body is attained. Without pause continue the movement by rotating the almost horizontal body to the left (circling right) and perform a face-vault left. Release the grasp of the left hand as the body passes over the horse and then swing the left arm sideways-upwards. Land with right side of body to horse and with the right hand still grasping the pommel. *Figs.* 48 A and B.

SHORT DESCRIPTION OF EXERCISE: *Toward standing: grasp pommels, spring to support and quarter-left body-turn with feint half-left circle of right leg over end of horse. Rock up and swing body around to the right to perform a face-vault left; finish in side standing with right hand grasping pommel.*

Teaching point: A feint circle is where one or both legs are passed over the horse without the hand grasp being removed.

13. *Starting position: Toward Standing.*

Grasp the pommels and, with a spring, swing the legs sideways-upwards to the left, at the same time making a quarter-left body turn. The grasp of the left hand is released as this is done and the body now occupies a piked posture above the horse with the body-weight supported by the right arm. The legs are parted and then drop astride the horse. Finish sitting astride the horse between the pommels. Now grip the rear pommel with both hands behind; take all the body-weight on to the arms; lean weight backwards over hands; swing the legs well up in front and perform a rear-vault dismount to the right. Finish in side standing with left hand resting lightly on the horse.

SHORT DESCRIPTION OF EXERCISE: *Toward standing: grasp pommels and rear-vault left to sit astride the horse between the pommels. Grasp pommel behind with both hands and rear-vault dismount to the right.*

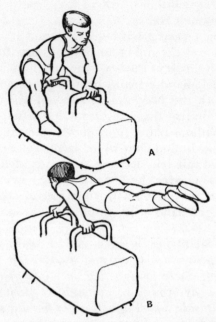

FIG. 48. (a) Feint rest left; (b) Feint rest left followed by horizontal face vault.

Teaching points: Practise first by facing the horse, placing the left hand on the end of the horse and grasping the left pommel with the right hand. Spring and swing legs to left and with a quarter-left body-turn sit astride the end of the horse. Dismount by grasping the pommel behind and performing a rear-vault to the right. This is quite a simple exercise – not nearly as complicated as it reads. Bear in mind when attempting the complete movement that as the legs drop from the pike or chair position the left hand, which has been removed for the passage of the right leg, quickly re-grasps the left pommel and helps to control the movement.

14. *Starting position: As for previous exercise.*

Grasp pommels and spring to support; commence a lateral body-swing and as the body swings to the left pass the right leg under the left and over the left pommel to the front of the horse. Continue circling the right leg to the right over the right pommel – removing the right hand for the leg to pass and finishing in the original support position.

SHORT DESCRIPTION OF EXERCISE: *Toward standing: grasp pommels and spring to support: right circle of right leg back to support position.*

Teaching point: Remember to swing the legs well up to each side and swing freely from the shoulders. Lean over to the left when swinging legs to the right and *vice-versa*.

15. *Starting position: Toward Standing, some two or three paces away from the Horse.*

Walk briskly forward, grasp the pommels and without pause, half-right circle of both legs over the left pommel, releasing the grasp of the left hand for the legs to pass, and finishing in back support. Pause in position then circle the right leg backwards over the right pommel (half-right circle right leg); half-left circle of left leg backwards over left pommel to join the right leg and finish in support position. Dismount with legs swinging backwards and pushing away with the arms.

SHORT DESCRIPTION OF EXERCISE: *Toward standing: grasp pommels; spring to support at the same time half-right circle of both legs over right pommel; half-right circle right leg; half-left circle of left leg to support and dismount with legs swinging backwards.*

Teaching points: Rhythmical swing and continuous movement.

16. *Starting position: Toward Standing.*

Grasp the left pommel with the right hand in overgrasp and place the left hand on the end of the horse. Now, with a spring, mount to support, taking most of the weight on to the right arm and at the same time making a half-right body-turn to back rest, grasping the free pommel with the left hand as the rest position is reached. Without pausing in position, swing the left leg backwards over the left pommel (half-left circle of left leg), again releasing the grasp of the left hand momentarily for the leg to pass. As soon as the left hand re-grasps, half circle the right leg backward over the right pommel, pass it under the left leg and over the left pommel back

to its original position (right circle of right leg). Without
pause, as soon as the right leg has completed its circle, circle
the left leg forward over the left pommel to join the right
leg so that a back rest position is again reached. Dismount by
swinging both legs forward and pushing away with the arms,
make a half-right turn and finish in side standing with right
hand grasping the right pommel.

SHORT DESCRIPTION OF EXERCISE: *Stand facing horse left
of centre grasping left pommel with right hand, left hand on
end of horse. With a spring and a half-left body-turn, mount
to back support. Now, half-left circle of left leg; full circle of
right leg; half-right circle of left leg: finish in back support;
dismount with a quarter-right turn.*

Teaching points: Practise the quarter turn mount to back
rest first, and when this has been mastered, add on the other
movements until the whole has been mastered.

17. *Starting position: Toward Standing.*

Grasp the pommels and vault to support at the same time
swinging the right leg forward over the right pommel (half-
left circle of right leg). Keeping the arms straight, practise a
lateral body-swing, allowing the legs to swing up high to each
side alternately and releasing the hand grasp of the hand on
the side to which the swing is being made. Now, when the
legs swing up to the left and at the high point of the swing,
change the relative position of the legs, passing the right leg
backwards under the left, and bringing the left leg forward to
the front. Continue the swing to the right and again change
the position of the legs, bringing the right leg forward over
the horse and passing the left leg backwards to the rear,
underneath the right leg. This movement can be carried on
continuously, and when carried out to the left with the left
leg being brought to the front from the rear it is called front
shears left. When performed with the right leg being brought
to front from rear in this scissors action the movement is called
front shears right. The sequence may be completed as follows.
When the left leg is in front bring it in tight against the horse
and then circle the right leg forward over the right pommel,
releasing the grasp of the right hand and making a quarter-
left body turn. As soon as the turn is completed, dismount to

land in side standing with left side of body towards the horse and the left hand still grasping the left pommel.

SHORT DESCRIPTION OF EXERCISE: *From forward astride position on the horse (right leg forward) lateral swing and forward shears left.*

Teaching points: Make a tentative approach by swinging legs to the left, bringing them together and stopping in side support on the horse. From this position part the legs again and allow them to swing downwards, re-grasping with the left hand after the legs have passed the pommel.

This is not a difficult movement – confidence is the most important factor – but remember to lean weight well over on to opposite arm when performing the shears.

18. As for the previous exercise but commence with the left leg to the front of the horse. Repeat the previous exercise and as the legs swing up to the left, bring the right leg forward over the horse, passing it under the left leg which is swung to the rear of the horse. This movement is called back shear left.

SHORT DESCRIPTION OF EXERCISE: *From support swing the left leg half-circle forwards: lateral swing and back shears left.*

Teaching points: The same points apply as for the previous exercise.

19. *Starting position: Toward Standing.*

Grasp the pommels with a combined grasp – the left hand in inward grasp and the right hand in reverse grasp, i.e. back of the hand facing inwards and elbow pointing out to the side. Now, with a spring, mount to support taking most of the weight on the right arm. At the same time circle the right leg forward over the right end of the horse. Keeping the right leg well elevated, make a half-right body-turn, releasing the grasp of the left hand and carrying the right leg right over the original left pommel to finish in single-arm support astride the right pommel. As this position is reached, place the left hand on the end of the horse and transferring most of the body weight to it, push away with the right arm and with a quarter-left turn dismount to side standing.

SHORT DESCRIPTION OF EXERCISE: *Toward Standing: Com-*

*bined grasp – left hand inward grasp, right hand reverse
grasp. Spring to support and with a half-left body-turn, pivoting on right hand, circle right leg over both pommels to take
up single-arm support on the right pommel. Place left hand
on end of horse and with a quarter-left turn, release grasp of
right hand and dismount to side standing.*

Teaching points: Practise the mount to single-arm support
first with a quarter-left turn and finishing in astride support.
Later, attempt the complete half-turn to single-arm support.
This exercise is not a very difficult one although it sounds
complicated.

20. *Starting position: Toward Standing to left of horse.*
Place the left hand flat on the left end of horse and grasp
the left pommel with the right hand in reverse grasp. The
right elbow has to be elevated and pointed outwards to do
this. Now, as in the previous exercise, mount to support on
the right arm, at the same time making a half-left body-turn
circling the right leg over the pommel and finishing in single-
arm support astride the left pommel – supported by the right
arm only. As the turn takes place the left arm is swung around
to grasp the free pommel and as it does so, the body-weight is
transferred from the right to the left hand. The right hand
grasp is momentarily released for the right leg to pass, and a
back support position is reached. Now, half-left circle of the
left leg followed by a complete right circle of the right leg;
half-right circle of left leg with a half-right body-turn, pivoting on the right hand, to place the left hand on the end of
the horse. Finish in front support with right hand grasping
left pommel and left hand on end of horse. Dismount with
legs swinging backwards with a quarter-right turn to finish
off in side standing, left hand resting on end of horse.

The foregoing will suffice to give beginners a fairly good
grounding in pommel horse work.

This is not intended to be an exhaustive list but should
serve as an introduction to the more advanced work of the
A.G.A. syllabus. Pupils who persevere and master these exercises will be amply rewarded whenever they decide to take
up pommel work seriously.